THE OPEN UNIVERSITY

Arts: A Third Level Course

Modern Art 1848 to the Present:
Styles and Social Implications

Units 15 and 16
ART SINCE 1945

Prepared by Michael Compton for the Course Team

The Open University Press

The Open University Press
Walton Hall Milton Keynes MK7 6AA

First published 1976

Designed by the Media Development Group of the Open University.

Printed in Great Britain by
COES THE PRINTERS LIMITED
RUSTINGTON, SUSSEX

ISBN 0 335 05156 1

This text forms part of an Open University course. The complete list of units in the course appears at the end of this text.

For general availability of supporting material referred to in this text, please write to the Director of Marketing, The Open University, P.O. Box 81, Walton Hall, Milton Keynes, MK7 6AT.

Further information on Open University courses may be obtained from the Admissions Office, The Open University, P.O. Box 48, Walton Hall, Milton Keynes, MK7 6AB.

1.1

Units 15 and 16   Art since 1945

These units cover the period of twentieth-century art subsequent to Surrealism.
I have started in the late 1930s when my first major artists began to find their way, but
the nominal period, 1945–76, is equal to that which includes developments from
Fauvism to the apogee of Surrealism, 1905–36, to which nine units have been devoted.
The number of movements in the two periods is similar but the number of individual
artists much greater in the post-1945 era, with the huge expansion of art schools,
museums and dealers' galleries. Moreover, you will have no help from George Heard
Hamilton's book; from Chipp a good selection of statements only for the first phase
and from Haftmann a poor selection of plates and one biased in a direction opposite
to my own.

In these circumstances I have chosen what I believe to be most characteristic of post-
war art, that is, the step-by-step elimination of various forms of personal, morpho-
logical stylization or distortion as a mode of expression; likewise, the elimination of
subtle and carefully adjusted arrangements of form and colour. For these, there has
been progressively substituted a preoccupation with the act and process of painting,
sculpting, etc., a preoccupation with the medium as such and with the extension of the
concept of medium to include the whole context within which the artist works.

The earlier units in this course were focused on Paris, with excursions to Russia,
Germany, Italy, Holland, etc. In my period the focus is on New York, with England
and the European countries producing many fine artists. Discounting every
pressure of American wealth, political hegemony and chauvinism, I think it true that
as much of the best work has been done there as in the whole of Europe, but more
important from my point of view is the fact that American artists have very often
produced the most single-minded and trenchant manifestations of any tendency or
preoccupation. It is easier, therefore, to use them as examples, as polar types. Indeed,
the first movement in the period, American Abstract Expressionism, can be said to
have been as great a catalyst for subsequent developments as Cubism had been at the
beginning of the century, thus shifting attention from Paris to New York. Of course
the American artists owed a great debt to Europe and not least to the wave of emigré
artists who fled to the United States about 1940.

The line of development is a fairly complex one but can be schematized as follows.
From Abstract Expressionism the violent brushwork is eliminated, but the concern
with the medium and process becomes central to the following generation of abstract
artists. At the same time American Pop art negates the element of indeterminism and
of abstraction, reintroduces the image, but in quotation. In British Pop style becomes
subject matter in itself. Minimalism shares the Pop use of predetermined forms and
processes but in an abstract manner; the predetermined scheme becomes more and
more evident to the point where the process of making can be discarded. This is one
element of the Conceptual Art that has been dominant for a decade; the other goes
back to Duchamp and to artists of the Pop generation, Jasper Johns, Klein, etc., who
used quotation and incorporation of objects and images to extend the scope of art into
direct intervention in the environment. Pop art is fairly equally divided between
England and America; Minimalism is largely American and Conceptual is divided
between Europe, including Britain, and America.

The most important omissions I have made are post-war Neo-Romantic and Neo-
Realist art, including Photo-Realism (which is an offshoot of Pop), a variety of artists
sometimes referred to as 'Image processors' (other than Jasper Johns), European
Painterly and Formal Abstraction including Neo-Constructivism and also the greater
part of American Formal or Hard-Edge Abstraction. Kinetic art, Happenings and

artists' film are left to be treated in the television programmes (TV 10 and 11) by Paul Overy. I have also omitted almost all the later work of artists who established themselves before 1940.

I must stress that, even in my own judgement, as many great artists and far more good artists, have been left out as are included. This has been especially agonizing since I know some of them personally and these and others are bound to find my choice both arbitrary and perhaps predictable. I have taken the decision to write mostly about individual artists and individual works of art (which are illustrated) rather than to talk broadly of isms and trends, although that might have allowed me to widen my scope. The reason for this is two-fold: first, that there are no other books to provide a background that could give reality to a generalized discussion (museums in this country are not well stocked with examples, nor are the works themselves very familiar); second, that new art tends to provoke a reaction as if it were a generalized gesture of subversion or even an insult, and I am convinced that it deserves as close an examination as anything in the past.

I have, generally, allowed the artists to state their own cases. For the second and larger part of my period this has to be in the form of a separate appendix, which takes the place of Chipp's anthology where he stops short. The statements on the whole are tactical and do not have the pretension to depth and universality which those of, say, Kandinsky or Mondrian do. This is partly the result of a growing distaste for such a mode of expression with its philosophical or even theological tone, but is also the effect of the use of the tape recorder and of the American cult of the informal. I have not often criticized such statements directly because I regard them as statements of intention or faith, rather than as justifications or explanations. In fact, they are sometimes curiously naive, a characteristic which consorts with the deliberate simplicity of the art they support.

Finally, I have not found room to write as much as I should about the political, social and economic background to the art. However, most readers will be familiar enough with the outlines of this; the chief factors have been, I think, the most obvious ones. On the one hand we have experienced rising standards of living, first in America and then, catching up, in Europe. The result has been not only more money to spend, more collectors, more museums, more artists (as I have said above) but also more and more education in fields like art and art history which are not directly necessary for material survival. The cult of art has progressed down the social and intellectual scale. Public response to fashion in art as in clothes and politics has been much quicker. On the other hand, there has been a crisis in confidence (as everyone knows or believes) in western capitalist values and in technology. There has been a very general trend to aestheticize social, political and even, I think, economic activity, since it has become harder to be certain about ends—the experience of action has replaced the goal. It is embarrassing to write such generalities but I hope that what follows will give some meaning to them.

Abstract Expressionism: Introduction

A glance at the illustrations in this unit (Figs 1, 4–7, 10–12, Plates 1–7) and in Haftmann (869–71, 881, 889–90, 896–901, 904–5, 907–10, 919, 942–43, 958, 963, 965) shows that, among its greatest artists, Abstract Expressionism was not a 'style'; a painting by Pollock does not resemble one by Newman in the way that a Monet and a Renoir were alike in 1870 or a Picasso and a Braque in 1911. On the other hand the painters were cohesive as a group and Abstract Expressionism is widely referred to as the most profound, the most influential and the most radical *movement* in post-war art.

In this section I will discuss the movement and some of its chief artists who are certainly among the greatest of their generation. But first a warning: once again do not take too seriously the name 'Abstract Expressionism'. This is a phrase that had been used of Kandinsky and is only one of several, including 'Action painting', 'Tachism' (from the French *tache*, 'brush-stroke') and 'American-type painting', that were proposed at the time. However, it is the one that has survived and become conventional even though the art has little in common with the various forms of German 'Expressionism' except a vigorous use of paint, and was not always 'Abstract', i.e. non-representational.

Second—a qualification. American Abstract Expressionism sprang largely from European roots and, in the period when it flourished, there also flourished in Europe many artists whose work, either springing from the same roots or influenced by events in America, resembles in certain ways that of the American artists. However the best of the American artists generally excelled their European contemporaries, whose work often appears as a compromise in comparison, and it is the achievement of the Americans that most radically affected the art that was to follow. I will be directing your attention to this group alone but you may wish to make your own comparisons and contrasts with the work of the Europeans illustrated in Haftmann.

Some names (grouped in order of country) are:
Bazaine, 822–24 and 826; de Staël, 834–38; Hartung, 873–76; Soulages, 877–79; Wols, 891–95; Mathieu, 906; Tàpies, 938; Saura, 882–83 and 885; Vedova, 884; Sonderborg, 887–88; Burri, 934; Jorn, 914; Davie, 950–51; Lanyon, 903; Hilton, 922. Paintings by the last three can be found in public galleries around Britain.
These are nearly all works of the 1950s when the American achievement was becoming widely known.

Abstract Expressionism 1: Prologue

During the 1930s in America as well as in Europe, the social and political consciousness of artists (like almost everybody else) was dominated by a succession of great events, recent or current: the 1914–18 war, the Russian Revolution, the Depression, the rise of fascism, the Spanish Civil War and the beginning of the 1939 war. Most of these naturally affected the subject matter of works of art and the attitudes of artists. However, the depression also produced institutions that directly affected the working lives of artists. The administration of President Roosevelt supported the arts by setting up official arts projects: these formed a part of the New Deal which included many schemes for spending public money to improve the economic base and human conditions as well as to maintain employment. In the arts the most important was the Federal Art Project (FAP), 1935–43, under the Works Progress Administration (WPA). During the thirties the WPA averaged more than two million men and women on its payroll including more than five thousand artists. The FAP paid artists like other workers, a wage of $24 for a twenty-four-hour working week, and they produced more than 108,000 easel paintings, 2500 murals and 1800 sculptures as well as prints and posters. There was virtually no quality test for inclusion in the scheme and therefore little stylistic exclusiveness. However, where works of art were to be publicly displayed, those who controlled the place had a say and could discriminate. The organizer, Holger Cahill, wrote:

> The organization of the Project has proceeded on the principle that it is not the solitary genius but a sound general movement which maintains art as a vital functioning part of any cultural scheme. Art is not a matter of rare masterpieces. The emphasis on masterpieces is a nineteenth century phenomenon. It is primarily a collector's idea and has little relation to an art movement.

There is no doubt that the great majority of artists who were associated with this project, including Gorky, Pollock, de Kooning, David Smith, Rothko and Louis, valued the experience highly. Firstly, the Project identified painting, sculpture and print-making as *work*, something worthwhile done for the community and deserving of a wage. Secondly, it was a gesture of the acceptance of the value of art to the state on a vast scale. Thirdly, it did not seek to use artists to celebrate the state in a crudely propagandist manner. Finally, and most important, it helped to establish strong art communities, especially in New York but also in other cities like Chicago. Artists' unions were formed in 1934 and, at the same time or later, a series of formal and informal artists groups, which met to discuss theoretical matters as well as conditions of work and survival. Although as in any group there have been schisms, to this day American artists will turn out to functions, discussions and manifestations of work, even when what is shown or said may be antipathetic to them personally. I believe that this has been among the factors which have given continued vitality to art there.

The association of artists working on the Project or making demands for the acceptance of their profession was reinforced by their unity in the face of fascism, and this in turn led them to try to evolve an American and democratic art. I hope to demonstrate the meaning of this later by quotations from the artists. There had already been a revival of regionalism both in subject matter and in style, whether rural or urban in focus. Now some artists identified anti-fascism with communism and found heroic examples in the work of the Mexican mural painters Rivera, Orozco and Siqueiros (Haftmann 805–9). WPA paintings are generally realist in style and show a preoccupation with farming or factory working or, like those of Rivera (Haftmann 805), with political allegory. The artists with whom this section deals either did not or quickly ceased to do that kind of painting.

Stuart Davis (Haftmann 820), one of the artists most committed to political and union action in the 1930s, wrote about state intervention (Appendix, p. 3). His association of state patronage with abstraction appears surprising, even disingenuous, but he was speaking with considerable knowledge of Russian and Nazi state patronage which favoured exactly the kind of art he condemned. What he is thinking of is state patronage in a democracy.

The relationship of the personal and formal concerns of an artist to his role in society will be discussed later, but first I want to deal briefly with the internal dynamic of the development of the movement. It happens that the vital traditions of modern western art as they affected the rise of Abstract Expressionism in America were literally embodied in individual artists: Arshile Gorky, Hans Hofmann and the wave of immigrant artists escaping the war and persecutions in Europe. The most important of these are listed by Chipp, p. 509. More than half the names are of Surrealists or of fantasists like Chagall but they also included late Cubist and abstract artists, among them Léger and Mondrian. Their influence replaced that of the realist Mexicans.

The European connection was also manifested in a series of temporary and permanent museums in New York including: Galatin's 'Museum of Living Art', 1927–43 (now at Philadelphia); the 'Société Anonyme', 1920–43 (now at Yale University); the Museum of Modern Art, founded in 1929, and the Museum of Non-Objective Painting, now the Solomon R. Guggenheim Museum, founded in 1937. In addition Peggy Guggenheim's gallery 'Art of this Century' exhibited both American and European Surrealists from 1942. The journals *VVV* and *View* published in New York supported Surrealism; *Art News* covered contemporary as well as old-master art. The scope of the Museum of Modern Art was the transition from Impressionism and Post-Impressionism through the subsequent movements very much as covered by this course. Its publications and exhibitions were definitive almost from the start under its great director Alfred Barr. The other collections were more idiosyncratic but represented the poles of formal abstraction and Surrealism very fully. In terms of permanent collections, exhibitions and information, this array easily exceeded anything that could be offered at the same date by institutions anywhere in the world.

HANS HOFMANN (1880–1966)

Hofmann was most important as a teacher. He came to America when he was in his fifties, having worked in Europe as a painter and teacher for many years and having been a friend and associate of many of the greatest European artists including Kandinsky and Matisse. The content of his teaching is adequately summarized in the text in Chipp, pp. 536–44. It will become clear later how much his ideas became the staple of other artists; I will only emphasize here the importance he gives to the medium, or, as he puts it, 'expression medium'. Not so obvious in this text, but implicit and also suggested by the phrase quoted by Chipp on p. 564 is the concept of the making of a work of art as a process of interaction with the medium rather than as simply a means to a predetermined end.

Hofmann used splashes and drips of paint in 1944 (Haftmann 905 is a later example). The significance of this technique (used earlier by the Surrealist Onslow Ford) is discussed later under Pollock. The painterliness (i.e. the free brush strokes and irregular forms) of Hofmann's abstraction clearly distinguishes it from the form of abstraction most current in America and represented by the American Abstract Artists' Association (see Haftmann 971 for a later example). This latter form of abstraction was regarded as academic by the artists I will be writing about and was based on harmonious relationships of flat colour areas, often bounded by black lines. It was strongly influenced by Mondrian who came to New York in 1940 and by the Abstraction-Création group in Paris.

ARSHILE GORKY (1904–48)

Stuart Davis wrote of Gorky:

> In the early part of 1934 the economic situation for artists had become so bad that they were forced to look around for ways and means to save themselves. They were shoved together by mutual distress and artist organizations of one kind or another began to form as a natural result. I was in these things from the beginning and so was Gorky. I took the business as seriously as the serious situation demanded and devoted much time to the organization work. Gorky was less intense about it and still wanted to play.

Irving Sandler, the historian of Abstract Expressionism, comments: 'By "play" Davis meant "paint".' (Sandler, 1970, p. 8). However Davis also said: 'The painting itself is the responsible social Act of the Artists and is one of the surest, most direct forms of communication known to man' (undated quote in Rose, 1967, p. 151), while Gorky in turn wrote of Davis:

> Has there in six centuries been a better art than cubism? No.
> Centuries will go past—artists of gigantic stature will draw positive elements from cubism.
> Clumsy painters take a measurable space, a clear definite shape, a rectangle, a vertical or horizontal direction, and they call it a blank canvas, while every time one stretches a canvas he is drawing a new space. How could they ever have understood cubism or the art of the twentieth century?
> (Gorky, 'Stuart Davis', 1931; see Chipp, pp. 532–33.)

Although this sentiment is not altogether original it makes two points: that art grows from the heroic achievements of the immediately previous age (Cubism) and that the painter is vitally concerned with the real space of the canvas and it is this rather than the arrangement of forms, colours, etc., that is the primary fact.

Gorky's development is a fairly complete recapitulation of the principal art achievement of the twentieth century, beginning with Cézanne. *The Artist and his Mother* (Fig. 1) is based on a photograph probably taken in Kharkom, Turkish Armenia, where he was born (Fig. 2). Look at the preparatory drawing (Fig. 3), one of several made for the painting. It is squared and numbered for enlargement onto the canvas and certain areas are much more highly finished than others. In this, as well as in its general style, it resembles Picasso's neoclassical drawings of the 1920s. (No good example is reproduced in the set books but the etching in Chipp, p. 411, indicates the type; see also Haftmann 563.) Those parts that are 'finished' are much more strongly marked and more active than the corresponding parts of the photograph: three of the four sleeves, the artist's hands and, to a lesser extent, the two heads.

Now return to the painting. It is first a statement of the artist's origins; the photograph on which it is based had been sent from home to Gorky's father, already a migrant to the USA. The painting focuses attention on the dark and intense eyes that for Gorky particularized his ethnic group, as do his mother's Armenian head dress and, to a lesser degree, his own shoes and fur collar.

The painting appears incomplete, although Gorky worked on it for about ten years (*c.* 1926–36). Other figure paintings including another version of this portrait have the same feature, and therefore there can be little doubt that it is intentional, but what is the effect of, or reason behind, it? The sleeves, which were the most highly defined three-dimensional elements of the drawing, are now almost the flattest; his mother's right arm and his own left, have become sequences of ogival curves and the area between them an equally active shape of very much the same type. The upper part of his mother's long apron (which is the busiest part of the photo) has become another

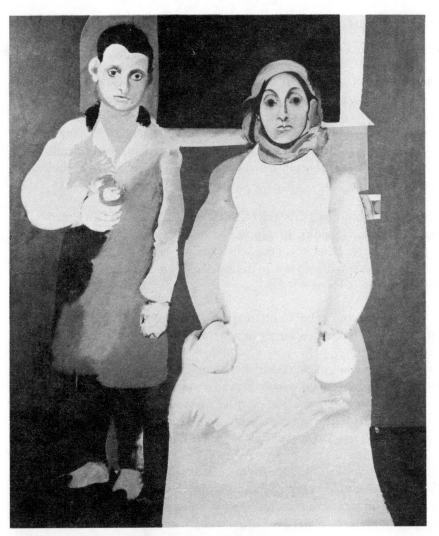

Figure 1 Arshile Gorky, *The Artist and his Mother*, 1926–36, oil, 60 × 50 ins (Whitney Museum of American Art, New York, gift of Julien Levy for Maro and Natasha Gorky in memory of their father).

Figure 2 Photograph of Gorky and his mother, Armenia 1912 (Mrs Sarkis Avedisian).

Figure 3 Arshile Gorky, *The Artist and his Mother*, drawing squared up, 1926/36, pencil, 24 × 19 ins (Estate of Arshile Gorky).

Figure 4 Arshile Gorky,
Organization, 1936, oil, 50 ×
60½ ins (Estate of Arshile
Gorky, courtesy of Mrs
Agnes Phillips).

Figure 5 Arshile Gorky, *Garden in Sochi I*, 1941, oil, 44¼ × 62¼ ins (Collection Museum of Modern Art, New York, Purchase Fund and gift of Mr and Mrs Wolfgang S. Schwabacher).

such shape, convex and concave curves producing sharp points which were to become a mark of his mature style. (He was later to paint a picture called *How my Mother's Embroidered Apron unfolds in my Life*). The apron appears to obliterate something that lies underneath. Though blank, therefore, it seems to lie on top. Consider this fact in relation to Gorky's remarks quoted above—about space on the canvas and about Cubism.

In spite of its unPicasso-like title, *Organization* (Fig. 4), *c.* 1934–36, is very close to some of Picasso's paintings of 1927–28 (the nearest example in the set books is the right-hand part of Haftmann 566). Gorky was deliberately setting out to identify with Picasso to learn from him, and pictures of this period have less of Gorky's 'hand-writing' in the forms than almost any others. However, even more than in earlier works he was investigating positive and negative space; forms and what lies behind or around them are interchangeable and make up the whole surface on an equal footing. The black lines are in thin paint and lie close to the surface, the voids between are built up with layer upon layer. In its complexity a self-contained form such as the one on the extreme left (like the sleeves in the portrait) could be either an object or the space between objects. Only the rounded forms (like the heads in the portrait) are unequivocally positive. This picture, in spite of its derivative character, is continuing to explore the basic problems of pictorial space and in a way more 'advanced' than its prototypes in Picasso. However he quickly reverted to curvilinear forms.

Figure 5, *Garden in Sochi I*, 1941, presents a new influence almost as strongly manifested—that of Miró. Read the statement Gorky made to the Museum of Modern Art which had bought a version of the picture (Chipp, pp. 535–36); this is written in a very different tone to the other texts. Like Figure 1, the painting recalls his childhood but in the manner of mythical fantasy. William Seitz (1962) identifies the tree with strips of cloth upper left and, tentatively, a porcupine, lower right. The blue rock, which is present in other versions lower left (Haftmann 942, but probably painted in 1942, after Fig. 5) is absent in this one. The whole picture is full of looping forms, the curves, concave and convex, meeting in points and again implying a reversibility of positive and negative (or figure and ground). The clearest case is the invasion of the dark central mass by a double curve (like a pair of breasts) but these, though apparently painted over it, are in the colour of the background. However, the mythic, poetic and erotic qualities of the painting (evoked in the statement in Chipp) are the most striking feature of the painting. 1941 was the date of his second marriage and 'Mougouch' in the text is his pet name for his wife. Equally important, it was the year of a great Miró exhibition and Gorky's close association with immigrant European artists soon followed. Some of these painters and writers, whose work he had admired passionately, became friends or colleagues. Most important for Gorky were the Surrealists Matta and Breton (the three artists whose stylistic influence on Gorky was strongest, Picasso, Miró and Kandinsky, were not among them). The effect on Gorky of the interest shown by these artists in his work and in the fact that they were present, talking and working in his own world, seems suddenly to have matured his art.

The Betrothal II (Plate 1), 1947, is an example of his mature style. It owes something to Kandinsky's paintings of 1912–14 (see Unit 10) in the episodic forms and the scumbled paintwork and to Matta in the tensely drawn lines and non-terrestrial space (compare Haftmann 939). The looping, ogival forms no longer raise the kind of ambiguity described above; instead, complementing the intense feeling evoked by the paintings, is a new formal characteristic: Gorky has brought into his paintings the features of his drawing. Line and colour are partially separated so that the colour areas do not quite end at the outlines. These paintings, therefore, make use of and assert the characteristic differences of the respective media: the drawn-out line expressing movement, acceleration and tension; the brushed colour expressing the activity of filling-in, expansion and obliteration. Both became fundamental elements of Abstract Expressionism in its central phase.

Exercise

Turn again to the paintings and drawing by Gorky (Figs 1 and 3–5, Plate 1 and Haftmann 942).

1   I have pointed out certain common features, some formal and some to do with subject or content. Look for others and try to describe the content and the features of *The Betrothal II.*

2   Consider these paintings in relation to the political preoccupations referred to by Stuart Davis (p. 9 and Appendix, p. 3).

Discussion

1   I have drawn attention to the element on the left of Gorky's *Organization* (marked with a small circle near the top) and related it loosely to the sleeves in *The Artist and his Mother*; a similar figure appears at the bottom centre of *The Betrothal II*. You may have read it as a leg and the central constellation as a figure, the 'bride'. There seems to be a second figure on the right, the groom, and on the left a squat figure, with a large head, perhaps a religious or legal official or witness. The recognition of figures gives extra intensity to the forms and to the wire-like drawing. Near the head of the bride, marked by a veil, is something which is at once a flower and a clawed paw like that of a bear or lion. The figure on the right can be identified without too much fancy as the painter carrying a palette but he too has flower-like or pod-like parts.

Compare this picture with *Garden in Sochi*: each has an upright form (a tree trunk?) at the centre top. The comparison is easier to see in the second version (Haftmann 942). This version and *Betrothal II* also have a configuration rising from a thin stalk to the right of this and both appear to have three main groups of forms, out of the centre of which the 'tree trunk' grows. There is an avowed erotic theme in each and a clear analogy between the two paintings. However, in *The Betrothal II* the playful mood of *Garden in Sochi*, a picture celebrating his marriage to 'Mougouch', has become tense to the point of acute pain. (In fact accidents, illness and a surgical operation had ruined his marriage and life; he committed suicide.) The hand-writing or typical shapes of the lines which appear in *The Betrothal II* can be found in all the earlier paintings except *Organization*, especially the parabolic intersecting curves already mentioned.

2   The political activity demanded of artists by Stuart Davis was in terms of joining the artists' union and campaigning for artists' rights but he expected the artist's work itself to be socially effective. In the instance of Gorky, then, one may say that the social act is:

(a) The public statement of his ethnic origins and of their enduring meaning to him.
(b) The willingness to bring in to the picture his most intense private feelings including his anxiety in relation to sex.
(c) The position that the artist must confront the work of his greatest immediate precursors and contemporaries and that this process is integral with the expression of private or public matter; an evolving world requires an evolving art.

Eventually Abstract Expressionism was promoted around the world as a manifestation of American freedom and individualism; conversely it became a principal butt of Russian satirists.

Abstract Expressionism 2: Heroic Phase

The 'heroic phase' of the movement may be considered to have begun in 1946 and was largely a New York phenomenon; the central artists came to maturity and achieved their most radical innovations together. In terms of immediate influence the most important were de Kooning and Pollock, and I will discuss several others, but there was a much larger group, of whom Gottlieb, Ferber and Motherwell are represented by statements in Chipp, who prints, in addition, part of an edited transcript of a discussion at a large gathering of artists. This kind of discussion was typical of the means by which ideas and attitudes were exchanged. That is, there is often passionate expression of attitudes but little about the practice of painting and less still about actual works of art. The photographs (Chipp, pp. 566–67) show that a high proportion of the major artists were present. Incidentally, it is clear from this and from other such documents that the artists had no difficulty in recognizing the quality of their colleagues.

WILLEM DE KOONING (born 1904)

The long statement in Chipp, pp. 556–61, is characteristic of de Kooning—it shows a state of mind anxious not to be explicit about the means, intentions or formal aspects of his painting. The last two pages seem to me the most interesting; they make it clear that he is hostile to the notion of style and to movements, which he sees as constraining forces determining the end product before working decisions have been made. He constantly asserts that painting, style and space are the act of living; and they also relate to his body: 'If I stretch my arms next to the rest of myself and wonder where my fingers are—that is all the space I need as a painter.' A statement made in 1944 quoted in the Appendix (p. 3) reinforces the same attitudes. The manner of his writing, like his painting, is full of jumps, apparent *non sequiturs* and ambiguities. He does not want to be pinned down, he wants to leave all options open, to be free to choose and for the choice to be serious, vital. His work will become what it is by choices—it will also be himself. His pictures are full of signs with multiple meanings. They are unfinished; they make visible the radical changes of mind of the artist, the evidence of his physical presence.

The *Seated Woman* of 1940 (Fig. 6) reveals the process of painting in many ways. There are, for example, at least three formulations of the woman's right leg, each on top of the other; curvilinear outlines, painted fields and areas defined by painting up to but not over them, alternate. The figure's left arm is slightly disjointed at the shoulder and the right is a characteristic looped shape that can only be read as an arm from its relationship to the body. De Kooning's paintings are full of highly personal shapes which he evolved and invented over a long period and which take their re-presentational meaning from relationships of this kind. They have a family resemblance to those of Gorky who was a close friend. In the black painting, *Dark Pond* (Fig. 7), 1948, these forms occupy virtually the whole of the picture. By painting predominantly in black, leaving narrow white intervals, de Kooning reverses the normal mode of drawing; this allows him the maximum of ambiguity of figure to ground. At the same time the black paint seems to obliterate almost the whole surface; there is no space left in it. The individual forms are similar to those which in other paintings might function as arms, shoulders or hips. He aims at the feeling of intimacy you have when looking at a part of the body very close to, so that out of scale and out of context, parts may be interchangeable—a finger is a leg. Here scale and context are denied because the context is entirely of other fragments, edge to edge.

This idea can be related to de Kooning's view of America as a 'no-environment'. He kept pinned up in his studio a newspaper photograph of a dense crowd of people filling the frame in such a way that it was not possible to place the event indoors or out of doors, or to tell what they were looking at : there was no context.

Figure 6 Willem de Kooning, *Seated Woman*, *c.* 1940, oil and charcoal on composition board, 54 × 36 ins (Philadelphia Museum of Art, gift of Mrs Albert M. Greenfield).

Figure 7 Willem de Kooning, *Dark Pond*, 1948, enamel on composition board, 46½ × 55½ ins (Collection of the Wiseman family, USA).

Figure 8 Willem de Kooning, photograph of *Woman I*, stage 4, 1950–52, oil, $75\frac{7}{8} \times 58$ ins (Collection Museum of Modern Art, New York).

Around 1950 de Kooning reverted to bright colours and moved away from abstraction, working on a series of paintings of women. Figure 8 shows *Woman I*, 1950–52, in a transitional state; Plate 2 is the completed picture. The picture was painted and repainted hundreds of times; bits of paper were laid over the canvas and painted, then removed or transferred to another place. Some of the signs of this remain in the painting: the woman's left arm is clearly a transposed leg, in other versions the breasts are eyes; the smile was originally a pasted-on mouth cut from an advertisement. The picture is powerful, vulgar, seductive; the looping curves and closed forms of the earlier paintings have almost entirely gone, replaced by splashes of paint.

By the mid 50s de Kooning was returning to abstraction (as he explains, he does not recognize a difference between figuration and abstraction). However *Suburb in Havana*, 1958 (Haftmann 900), remains clearly a landscape. The brush strokes are now even larger in relation to the canvas size and space is more clearly described by the direction of the gesture. Closed forms have entirely disappeared.

Exercise

1   Read again the short quotations in the Appendix and relate them to *Woman I*.
Note down as many ways as you can find in which the picture is 'unfinished'.
2   De Kooning has often been described as a late Cubist: briefly note any resemblances you can find between *Woman I* and a Cubist painting such as Picasso's
Portrait of D H Kahnweiler (Haftmann 168).

Discussion

1   Most obviously the image is barely suggested by dashes of paint which do not
completely enclose forms; similarly, areas of colour remain brush strokes and leave
underlying colours showing through. There are alternative positions for the same part
of the body, for example, two right hands. All this suggests that the painting is the
static remains of a violent activity which could be resumed at any time.
2   *Woman I* shares with Cubist pictures the fact that it is simply a figure treated as a
still life—there is no activity or anecdote in the subject itself. Although analytic, both
paintings clearly do violence to the subject; both paintings comprise overlapping and
fragmentary planes, loosely knit into a figure. Line and plane do not always coincide
and have a degree of independent significance. Both pictures have a shallow box-like
space; a degree of depth is suggested by the overlapping of planes and by diagonals.
The figure and the background interpenetrate.

JACKSON POLLOCK (1912–56)

On the basis of his painting between late 1946 and 1950, together with a smaller number of pictures from 1943–46 and 1951–55, Pollock ranks very highly among the most
radical and most powerful painters of the post-war period. His few recorded statements (little of interest can be added to Chipp, pp. 546–48) are clear and relevant, but
the most specific and independent (1947) deals only with the act of painting, not with
aims or interpretation. This was a conscious decision, for the draft of the statement
included the sentence: 'The source of my painting is the unconscious.' This mirrors
the phrase in the statement of 1944 and must refer to the concept called by Breton
'psychic automatism' (Chipp, p. 412; see also Unit 14). Pollock's personality, his
concern with the unconscious, the techniques he evolved and his formal innovations
are very closely interlinked. Pollock fluctuated between acutely depressive periods,
alcoholic binges and intensely creative bursts; the period 1947–50 was his only prolonged respite from alcoholism.

In 1937–40 he had undergone psychotherapy, for the last two years with a young
Jungian analyst. By this time, according to the analyst (Dr Henderson), Pollock was
already interested in the Surrealist doctrine of psychic automatism. The analysis
was carried on largely by means of drawings which Pollock showed to the doctor;
these drawings are a vivid anthology of mask-like heads, distorted and convoluted
animals, humans and chimeras, ritualistic events and totemic symbols. It can be
presumed that he offered them as a means of demonstrating what was in his unconscious; but with all their apparently uncontrolled energy, they often show the
influence of artists like Picasso or Masson and a knowledge of primitive, especially
North American Indian, art forms. The drawing reproduced (Fig. 9) includes a
bestial head, perhaps a bull, with its nostrils and a closed mouth lower left, a snarling
mouth left, and another with bared teeth and a fluttering tongue like a bunch of
feathers. On the right, lines interweaving energetically almost at random, materialize
a figure, but below, a little skein of lines (or a single line) weave a calmer rhythm but
no image. These are hardly more than doodles, but, like many details of the
drawings, prophetic of what was to come.

Turn now to *Pasiphae* (Haftmann 896). This is a fairly large picture by the standards
of the time, 54 × 96 ins, and since it was not a decoration, was clearly intended to be a

Figure 9 Jackson Pollock, drawing presented to Dr Henderson for analysis, coloured pencil on paper, $9\frac{3}{4} \times 8\frac{1}{4}$ ins (Maxwell Galleries Ltd, San Francisco).

major 'statement' by the artist. Pollock had worked with the muralist Thomas Hart Benton and this may account in part for the fact that many of his paintings, even at this time, are larger than most of the work of, say, Ernst, Masson or Miró. Like Gorky, Pollock is elevating the intensely personal to the scale of the public. (A reason for this may lie in Jung's notion of the universality of symbols and the public expression of the common unconscious in ritual.) This picture was originally called *Moby Dick* by Pollock and renamed at the suggestion of a writer *Pasiphae*. Nevertheless it does not appear to refer directly either to the legend of the whale or the bull. Two tall figures can be distinguished at each end, standing the full height of the canvas. Between them in a barely discernible wide oval lies an animal, its bear-like legs to the right, a multiple head, like the one described in the drawing, to the left. At either end of the oval appear to be supports which suggest the structure of an altar and hence an image of sacrifice. Along the belly of the animal are three clearly marked pale blue oval shapes suggesting the breasts of a she-wolf (the title of a closely related painting). The apparent violence of the brush strokes, for example the black zigzag over the body of the animal, seem to express both the violence of the event and of the artist's feelings which are, of course, one, since the event is interpreted as such in the mind of the artist.

There is hardly any sense of foreground or background; the space is almost entirely filled up with the results of the intense activity of the artist. Moreover the ambiguity which Pollock seeks to establish in the reading of his figures (compare the description of the drawing above) involves opening them up to what is around them, so that parts can be, as it were, exchanged with neighbouring figures or space. By figure, here, I do not mean necessarily human or animal, but anything that can be seen or interpreted as an entity. This is also true of many Analytical Cubist paintings (such as Haftmann 168 and 177) but it is clear that Pollock is very far away from those artists in his intention and state of mind; nevertheless the formal effect of the network of ambiguities is the same—to knit together the whole surface.

One, 1950 (Plate 3), was painted in the manner described by Pollock in Chipp, pp. 546–48, and can be seen hanging on the wall behind the artist working in the photograph in Chipp, p. 547.

Exercise

Consider how *One* is related to and goes beyond *Pasiphae* in the terms in which I have described the latter.

Discussion

Most obviously it seems to be entirely abstract—no symbolic or archetypal figures can be discerned. However, the idea of automatism is even more completely achieved. Without any figures, this automatism seems to reach towards the physical rather than the psychic. By omitting a reference to the unconscious in the statement quoted, Pollock laid emphasis on the physical, especially in the first and second paragraphs. There is, however, a reference to Indian sand painters (whose work is part of a ritual) and the third paragraph expresses a theory of the mutual relationship of the sub-consciously directed artist working literally in and reacting to his painting as it progresses. Since the artist is not acting towards a predetermined result but responding to the results of his own activity, there can be, as he says in the third quotation (of 1951), 'no accident, no beginning and no end'. There can also be no representation and no abstraction in the sense of figures in significant relationship for both of these involve specific intentions.

Pollock's method of working freely all round a canvas lying on the floor is also obviously linked to the disappearance of images. Although it would be possible for a highly disciplined artist, it is hardly thinkable that a more instinctive one could paint a standing figure upside down or from the side. As Chipp's photograph shows, Pollock worked on a roll of canvas and determined the edges afterwards. The relationship of the painting to the canvas is therefore not the filling up of a given rectangle (compare this with Gorky, p. 9) as it is in *Pasiphae*. Also the lack of division of the canvas into figure and ground is even more complete than in *Pasiphae*. This derives from the fact that the paint is trickled in long, curving lines or small splashes, which do not, cannot even, delimit forms. Although many of the marks are elongated, the evident traces of the irregular fall of the paint prevent one from interpreting them as lines, but Pollock in this picture is also careful to prevent the occurrence of closed forms. In spite of its all-over effect this picture, like all of his paintings, has a clearly marked rhythm. This can be seen most easily in the long, flattish arcs of black paint, running mostly up and down the canvas. This is counterpointed by other colours which tend to have their own separate rhythms: the thin white lines, more hesitant and often dominantly horizontal, the blue and pink in small splotches and the aluminium (which appears grey in the photograph) in larger and more diffuse blots. Not easily visible in the photograph is the fact that the type of blot or line is related to the viscosity of the paint and a close examination reveals that it is possible to trace the order in which one paint mark has been superimposed on another. The transition from the use of a brush to poured or dripped paint reduces the sense of physical violence (expressing an emotional state) for the dynamic of the former was a stabbing, slashing one and in the latter the muscular movements are exercised through a medium which has no rigidity.

Figure 10 Jackson Pollock, *Blue Poles*, 1953, oil, Duco and aluminium paint on canvas, 83 × 192½ ins (National Gallery of Australia, Canberra).

Blue Poles, 1953 (Fig. 10 and Plate 4), and *Scent*, 1955 (Haftmann 899), follow a period in which Pollock had experimented with a reversion to figure painting rather in the manner of the small figure on the right of Figure 9. Leaving aside the eight 'poles' themselves, *Blue Poles* contains a very much larger number of almost straight lines; many of these are white. On the right they are nearly parallel and vertical, forming a screen in the 'middle distance' of the painting that rises from the bottom edge. On the left they appear at the same level but are crisscross and more random. Pollock generally chose a colour and then used it more or less densely over the whole canvas, making a repeated mark with it. He would then choose another combination of colour, rhythm and means (pouring, dripping, trickling from a stick, etc.) and go over the picture again. One may see, therefore, the same colours and rhythms appearing in the same sequence of superimpositions all over the picture (see the detail illustrated as Plate 4). This effect is analogous to the 'levels' used by archaeologists to describe the chronology of an excavated site. The element of process or autobiography in these works by Pollock is read in the same manner; that is, there are two kinds of implied time in his pictures: the superimposition of layers just described and the effect of lateral movement, rhythm, speed or acceleration that the thickness, scatter, texture and curvature of lines convey. Both of these can be seen in the paint itself and therefore may be thought of as 'evidence' and not as 'illusion'.

It is Pollock's achievement that he should have invented a mode of painting that was so completely abstract—referring not to the visible world nor to the conventional mental world of geometry—but which was so completely real; the paint is nothing but paint. In *Blue Poles* he was again turning from representation to abstraction but the straight lines of the poles, however often they may break up into random splotches or be broken into and violated by other colours, seem to represent an assertion of the will, like the grid of lines already described. However, there seems to be a degree of desperation in the device, as if he had lost the power of effortless control that gives an order to the paintings of the late 1940s in spite of the apparently random surface. If this is so, Pollock's use of chance has a different character from the theatrical serendipity of most Surrealist paintings based on automatism.

Abstract Expressionism 3: Rothko, Still, Newman and Louis

The four painters in this section are of similar quality and influence to Gorky, de Kooning and Pollock but are treated more briefly here. Three of them came to maturity about 1948; their subsequent work does not vary greatly but encompasses a very wide range of expression within an apparently limited range of means. The thought expressed by Mark Rothko and Adolph Gottlieb as point 4 in Chipp, p. 545, is true of all of them; true also in a way of Pollock, in spite of the complexity of his surfaces. Point 5 is also important and relevant; for all the American artists mentioned here, subject matter is crucial. Rothko and Gottlieb use the term where we might now expect the word 'content', but their reference to what is 'tragic and timeless' *versus* '. . . pictures of the American scene . . .' shows that they do indeed mean subject matter, which I may define briefly as that to which the artist turns his attention, as distinct from content, which I take to be the entire significance of the work of art in the widest context. All four artists attempt to produce paintings which are unitary and decisive and which defy analysis into parts and into relationships between parts. The parts that the paintings do have and the relationships between them are very simple and may be perceived at first glance. You will find that the same is true of the next generation of American artists (see, for example, Stella and Judd, pp. 61–64); indeed it tends to be an ambition of most American artists. I have always thought of their cult of the single decisive act as being related to the ritual shoot-out at the end of a conventional 'western' or 'private-eye' film.

The four artists represent very different temperaments, from the dominant emotionalism of Rothko to the visual sensuousness of Louis and from the belligerence of Still to the shining clarity of Newman. But it is the directness of their method that gives such great strength to the result.

MARK ROTHKO (1903–70)
(Read Chipp, pp. 548–49.)

Rothko constantly emphasizes that his pictures are like dramas and rituals; he refers often to actors and to their gestures. Elsewhere he said: 'It was with the greatest reluctance that I found the figure could not serve my purposes . . .' The reason is perhaps given near the bottom of p. 549 of Chipp: '. . . the [painted] solitary figure could not raise its limbs in a single gesture . . . nor could the solitude be overcome . . .'. The reference to solitude is also characteristic. For Rothko this was an intense and, I believe, constant experience, but he also sees it as liberating—see the second paragraph of Chipp, p. 548. *Red, White and Brown*, 1957 (Haftmann 963), is a characteristic painting of his mature period. The size of the picture (about 102 × 84 ins) is important—related to the human figure, but just too large for a person to stand and reach the sides and top. Read the quotation in the Appendix, pp. 3–4; the intimacy Rothko speaks of is the complete absorption of the viewer into the painting—the overwhelming revelation which attains to a sense of complete identity. The formal characteristics of the paintings are entirely in accord with such an aim.

Vessels of Magic (Fig. 11) is an earlier painting, contemporary with the statement in Chipp; it is clearly influenced by 'biomorphic' Surrealists such as Miró, Matta or Tanguy. There are certainly actors, although not human. They seem to float in an almost empty space limited by a horizon—they have a primitive, magical or ritual character. Formally, the ground is painted in horizontal strokes—the figures predominantly vertical—both are generally transparent and imprecise. The five figures are almost symmetrically placed, like the figures in a fifteenth-century altarpiece, but there is also a second, loose symmetry about a horizontal line, as if the lower part were the reflection of the upper in the surface of a sheet of water.

Figure 11 Mark Rothko, *Vessels of Magic*, 1946, watercolour, 38¾ × 25¼ ins (Courtesy of the Brooklyn Museum, New York).

By 1950, personages of this kind have been replaced by rough rectangles of colour but they remain expressive individuals. From this time on there is always a near-perfect lateral symmetry and often an approximate vertical symmetry, as in *Red, White and Brown*. The role of this symmetry can be understood from Rothko's repeated statements that his pictures were not to be regarded in terms of relationship but in terms of expression, and also from his remarks about scale. No painting which contains more than one colour or shape can be without relationships, but the use of symmetry reduces the interest of them and their power (in this case) to distract the viewer from the principal expressive role of the elements. Similarly the areas of colour here are hardly more than zones of the canvas; the paint sinks into the surface like a dye, reducing any sense of independent reality. The colour areas do not touch or overlap and their simplicity reduces the number of relationships that can be considered. Although some may seem to recede and others to advance there is no tension between them because they are isolated from each other and from the edge of the canvas. (This is more strictly true of Rothko's work from about 1956 but it is developing from 1950.) The vertical axis of symmetry places the viewer directly in front of the picture—the intimate and at the same time ritual relationship towards which Rothko strives.

Rothko perhaps went further than any other artist in making painting the vehicle for the direct expression of feeling envisaged by Schopenhauer and Kandinsky (discussed by Peter Vergo in Radio programme 5), but he recognized that spatial relationships are no substitute for the temporal relationships of music. Except where a strongly inculcated habit exists, like that of reading lines of print on a page, the eye does not scan in a predictable way and therefore a painter, unlike a writer or a musician, does not create a sequence of events. A painter's events are essentially simultaneous although, if he can hold the attention of a viewer for long enough, he can cause a feeling to develop over a period. A symmetrical painting is perhaps most likely to do this; many of the world's contemplative icons, such as the crucifix and the mandala, have this form. Feelings do not occupy space but are experienced as global, if changing and insubstantial. The sense of floating in water or space is a pictorial equivalent of this and dictates the size of painting which must be large enough to fill the field of vision.

CLYFFORD STILL (born 1904)

Still's character and aspirations are trenchantly expressed in the text in Chipp, pp. 574–76. He is saying, in his way, what all his contemporaries said: that art is of the highest importance, that the artist must be free of compromises as well as of tyrants, that this freedom must characterize the way he works, so that the careful balancing of parts is as unworthy as the fruitless attempt to imitate; and that to work within a style is to deny oneself freedom and responsibility.

Haftmann 908 and Plate 5 are fairly typical of his work from 1946. Symbolic of the freedom asserted by Still is the manner in which areas of paint seem to have grown over the surface of the painting, stroke by stroke. This appears both from the character of the edges which remain and from the (usually) heavily brushed or trowelled texture which can be seen in even such a small reproduction as Haftmann 908. The effect of the edges is often that of the kind of layering that is seen in the grain of wood or the weathering of geological strata. Adjacent or superimposed colour areas seem to match one another, sometimes closely, as on the left of Plate 5, and sometimes at a distance, as upper right. Many paintings are executed with predominantly vertical brush strokes, as here, and this determines the character of the growth and the final breakdown of the momentum of an area at its edges; it produces the parallelisms just mentioned. The overall effect is frequently one of the conflict of one mass against another for dominance of the area.

BARNETT NEWMAN (1905–70)

Like Still, Rothko and Pollock, Newman was contemptuous of the abstract art of arrangement.

> The present feeling seems to be that the artist is concerned with form, colour and spatial arrangement. This objective approach to art reduces it to a kind of ornament.
> (Barnett Newman, 'The Plasmic Image', c. 1943–45; published in Hess, 1971.)

Later he wrote:

> I am always referred to in relation to my colour. Yet I know that if I have made
> a contribution it is primarily in my drawing. . . . Instead of using outlines, instead
> of making shapes or setting off spaces, my drawings declare the space. Instead of
> working with the remnants or space, I work with the whole space.
> (Seckler, 1962, pp. 83, 86–87.)

Newman's statements, Chipp, pp. 550–52, represent the strength of the conviction
of the primacy of subject matter of an artist whose work appears to many to be no
more than a division of colour and space. His own resolution of this paradox is contained in 'The First Man was an Artist', Chipp, pp. 551–52, where he identifies the
aesthetic act with the attempt to attain to the unknowable, and later he identifies this
with the sublime (Chipp, pp. 552–53).

Onement I, 1948 (Fig. 12), was the first painting in which Newman attained to the
kind of art he had been writing about for some years. The canvas is covered with an
even field of dark red and, over this, down the centre, is painted a rough-edged
vermilion stripe, or 'zip', as he called it. The stripe, because it is central and built up
in thick paint, stands as a figure or totem—not as a line dividing the canvas. It is like
the figure 'one' and is alone and complete, the 'onement' of the title which also refers
to sexual union. *Vir Heroicus Sublimis*, 1950–51 (Plate 6), is again a red canvas and is
divided by five narrow 'zips'. The variation in colour and width of the zips, and the
fact that they run from top to bottom, makes each divide the whole canvas. This gives
a meaning to Newman's claim to have innovated in drawing and to be working with

Figure 12 Barnett Newman,
Onement I, 1948, oil, 27 × 61
ins (Courtesy of Mrs Annalee
Newman).

the whole space; it also demonstrates the essential difference between his art and that of the greatest maker of 'Form, colour spatial arrangements', Mondrian (see Unit 12). Mondrian also painted stripes and areas of flat colour but virtually every line has another at right angles to it so that they delimit a rectangle within the rectangle of the canvas. Curiously the only feature of Mondrian's paintings that 'declares' the whole space in Newman's sense is the uncrossed gap between two vertical, parallel lines in certain pictures of 1935–40.

That two stripes are alike and two nearly alike (the white ones) implies alternate overlapping divisions, but the field itself does not vary in colour between the stripes, as it does in some of Newman's other paintings. In *Vir Heroicus Sublimis*, unlike *Onement I*, the zips are sharp-edged and fine (sometimes he used both kinds of stripes in one painting). The picture is very large, nearly eighteen feet wide; Newman indicated in an exhibition that he wanted visitors to approach such a picture closely, evidently so that it would fill the whole field of vision. In the centre field is a square, but this is not obvious because the edges are marked by different coloured zips. For Newman, choice in painting was not continuous or recurrent as it has been described for other Abstract Expressionist painters, but was a matter of coming to a decision about the colours and, above all, the proportions which place the zips. These proportions may have had cabalistic significance but the choice was neither arbitrary or simply a matter of taste.

MORRIS LOUIS (1912–62)

Louis can be considered as the last of the major Abstract Expressionist painters. He worked in studied seclusion in Washington, rarely visiting New York, rarely looking at other artists' work and refraining even from keeping his own pictures where he could see them in case they should, as he said, 'get in his eye'; that is, prejudice his continuing powers of invention.

However one decisive experience was seeing in 1954 a painting by Helen Frankenthaler, *Mountains and Sea*, in which the paint was thinned so as to sink almost entirely into the canvas as a stain or dye. You can see this effect on a less grand scale in Plate 4. Following this event, Louis rapidly evolved a new means of painting and a series of ideas that raised him to the quality and rank of his greatest contemporaries (Plate 7).

Louis painted on canvases hung over or stapled to simple wooden frameworks. He worked in a small room which meant that larger canvases had to be folded and he could not see the whole of them at one time; the canvas fell loosely from the framework like a curtain. He used sponges soaked in very thin paint which, when applied to a canvas, would run down it spreading laterally somewhat and taking a direction which could be controlled by varying the viscosity and quantity of the paint and by pulling away the foot of the canvas to alter its slope. In terms of its directionality this is a form of drawing but, even more clearly than in the case of Pollock, it is a form of drawing that does not delimit objects or spaces. The effect of the staining was to identify the colour with the canvas; it is not layered. Where colours overlap they fuse physically and optically but the limits of each separate stain remain visible as a change of hue (Haftmann 910). The application of successive overlapping stains of a wide variety of bright colours (which can often be seen at the edges) may produce a dark veil; if the colours are few or closely related the veil may be brilliant.

Most of Louis's paintings demonstrate a preoccupation with the edges as well as with the field of the canvas. All of these considerations show that the physical properties of pigment, medium and canvas were central to Louis's concept of art. Unlike the other artists described, it is impossible to designate a content to his art outside of these; Louis wrote nothing about his art and most of the titles were given to the paintings by others. The value he attached to the activity of painting, an activity which takes its force and meaning from the developing history of art as well as from the artist's own powers and perceptions, is the nearest thing to content that can be attributed to him.

Exercise

I have referred to the *scale* of paintings by Rothko, Still, Newman and Louis. Write
notes on the effect or implications of large size in abstract painting.

Discussion

It is difficult to see such pictures as portable 'windows on the world' in the way that
smaller paintings can be seen, especially if framed (even Mondrian's and Malevich's
paintings are windows onto an ideal world); it is also difficult to see them as decorative
or precious objects. They therefore share with frescoes the character of being environmental, aspiring to establish the emotional state of the room in which they are placed.
It is often hard to hang several successfully in one room, especially if they are by
different artists.

If a painting is very large, especially if it is very long and you are fairly close to it, you
have to move about to see it all. This effect reinforces its environmental character. A
very large picture requires the artist to move about and treat the painting as an
'environment' in which he has to work, rather than as an object to be manipulated.

The effect of a colour is much stronger if the area is very large. Indeed, if a painting
is not about relationships between coloured forms, the size and hue of these forms are
the main things that the artist has to work with. In the extreme case of monochrome
paintings (see Yves Klein, p. 40) these are, with texture, the *only* things he has to
work with.

A very large picture is often an indication that a painter feels he has something
especially important to present to the world. It generally implies a public, rather than
a private, mode of expression and may represent a heavy commitment in materials by
the artist to a work which may be extra difficult to sell.

You may feel that many abstract works are overextended. The artist is aware that this
is a possible reaction and that the choice of a large format is a risk; this again implies a
strong commitment on his part. Louis, in Plate 7, emphasizes this danger by leaving
the whole centre and upper part of his painting empty, forcing the attention of the
viewer to the act and the significance of the slanting bands of colour at each side of
him.

Sculpture

Sculpture is completely unrepresented in Haftmann and post-war sculpture in Hamilton. There are, therefore, no plates in the set books to support what can be included here. Moreover, what we do have room for is quite inadequate to give a connected account of the development of the art in the whole period. But the problem is mitigated by the fact that, apart from a very small number of outstanding individuals who had mostly established their ways of making art in the thirties, up to about 1960 sculpture remained generally derivative of painting and of lower quality.

Two outstanding artists, Henry Moore and Alberto Giacometti, describe their attitudes to their art and their way of working very clearly in Chipp (pp. 593–601). Their direct influence on the sculptors described in this section has not been great, but I will deal very briefly with them, because they do, I believe, epitomize the state of sculpture in the period immediately after the war.

Both sculptors are primarily concerned with the human figure; both are also concerned with the relation of figure to the surrounding space and, it seems to me, with the point at which an image becomes sufficient—sufficient, that is, to be read or responded to as a figure. Perhaps for this reason, each of them often produces figures that seem to have suffered, or are under threat of attrition or dissolution. The morphology of these figures, however, could hardly be more different.

Figure 13 Henry Moore, *Three Piece Reclining Figure, No. 2 Bridge Prop*, 1963/64, bronze, 99 ins long (City Art Galleries, Leeds).

Moore adheres to the monumental tradition (Fig. 13). His figures are often heroic in scale and ambiguous in their mode of expression: a single form may represent a lying woman and a mountain, a broken bone and a head. The power of the metaphor may depend on a sense of disparity between actual and original scale, or between actual and suggested scale. For example, a (modified) small bone may be enlarged to stand for a torso or the form of a small flint may seem to represent a great rock.

In the case of Giacometti (Fig. 14) the vital sense of space around or between the figures also depends on our reading of the figures and their gestures, the most important of which may be a rigid stillness. In both artists, therefore, the 'poetry' of the work is dependent first of all on a recognition of a subject or multiple subject.

Moore also represents a very ancient tradition of sculpture in which three-dimensional forms are perceived as silhouettes that are constantly modulated as you explore them. The photograph of Moore working, on p. 594 of Chipp, shows that the fall of light and shadow creates a secondary linear counterpoint, which both pleases the viewer and reveals more of the form. Moore's drawings confirm that he uses line and texture to define surface, surface to define volume and volume to suggest mass. In addition he may discover forms and associations in his materials, as he works on or contemplates them rather than impose them. It is from this tradition, a tradition that descends from Michelangelo, that Smith and Caro stand apart and have implicitly contradicted in their work.

DAVID SMITH (1906–65)

Smith was trained as a painter and shared many of the interests and experiences of the Abstract Expressionists. His sculpture grew out of the canvas in the literal sense that it began as relief and collage; throughout his career his sculptures tend to have a front and a back, like paintings, and to include found elements. Such found objects may have a specific function in the culture, like tools, or be stock materials, like offcuts of steel, or be stock concepts, like rectangles, cubes and cylinders. The basic work processes are not carving and modelling but bending rods, cutting out profiles and welding together sequences of elements. Although Smith was friendly with some of

Figure 15 David Smith, two *Tank Totems*: left: *Tank Totem IV*, 1953, steel, 92½ × 33⅜ × 29 ins (Albright-Knox Art Gallery, Buffalo, New York); right: *Tank Totem III*, 1953, steel, 84½ × 27 × 20 ins (Artist's collection) (Group photograph courtesy of the Archives of American Art, David Smith collection).

Figure 16 David Smith, group of three *Cubi*: left: *Cubi XVIII*, 1964, stainless steel, height 92 ins (Museum of Fine Arts, Boston, anonymous donation); centre: *Cubi XVII*, 1963, stainless steel, height 84 ins (Dallas Museum of Fine Arts); right: *Cubi XIX*, 1964, stainless steel, height 89 ins (Tate Gallery, London) (Group photograph courtesy of the Archives of American Art, David Smith collection).

the painters, he lived outside New York with a workshop full of metal scrap and stock in a landscape filled with his accumulating work. He had an affinity with large machinery and liked to project himself as a workman (see the photograph in Chipp, p. 578).

Smith worked in series of related sculptures, often on several series at once. Figures 15 and 16 show members of such series; all five sculptures demonstrate his continuing references to the body. The earlier group shows clearly the echo of the Picasso–Gonzalez and Gonzalez welded sculptures that were the primary formative influence on Smith from the thirties. You will also notice that they stand directly on the ground, with only a vestigial base or none at all, although there are elements included in the sculptures which are clearly differentiated as supports. In the 1953 group they have the character of legs; in the 1960s group, of columns. The title *Tank Totems* refers to the incorporation of concave discs, made for the ends of tanks or boilers. They appear cut in half on the sculpture on the left, whole on the right.

Exercise

Now read the statement by Smith in Chipp, pp. 576–77 and the review by Kramer, Chipp, pp. 583–85. Considering the illustrated sculptures, expand or comment on Kramer's remarks in the last five lines of p. 584 and the first seven lines of p. 585.

Discussion

The Surrealist element is easiest to see in the two *Tank Totems*. The unexpected juxtaposition of parts, the totemic idea itself and the final character of the 'beast' or 'personage' that the sculpture assumes are all common features of Surrealism. There is a particular ambiguity in the existence of three legs: is it man, animal, or tripod? The element of expressionist gestural freedom seems to me to be absent from these works, as it is from most of Smith's. The freedom is rather one of juxtaposition and association, but it is also Cubist. This is the syntax referred to by Kramer and described by Smith in the middle of his three paragraphs: the part, the unit of parts and the whole; word, phrase and sentence. His doctrine of after-images is obscure; it seems to be equivalent to the generalized experience of the part and stands in relation to the part rather as the meaning of a word stands to the word itself, except that here there can be no simple dictionary definition. It is a substitute for representation and, as such, functions like the elements of a Cubist painting. As in a Cubist painting the parts are partially isolated and self-contained—not fused, but touching and overlapping. They do not describe or comprise a surface, and space is left open between them. Even in the group of *Cubi*, although the elements are solid they are deployed in the shallow space of a Cubist painting. Here, too, the elements are built-up in a manner which seems to defy gravity, as forms in a painting may. Voids can be as significant as solids, as they are in the figure–ground relationship. The frame within the left-hand sculpture of Figure 15, through which the photographer has caught the horizon, may be seen as equivalent to the kind of *trompe-l'oeil* element found in some Cubist painting.

The effect of a photograph is to flatten and freeze an object into a relationship with its surroundings. In the case of Smith, who liked to place his pieces out of doors, this is not too damaging; the earlier sculptures are flat and linear, sometimes appearing as if drawn on the background against which they are seen. The *Cubi* are constructed in stainless steel with the surfaces roughened so that they take on the colour of their surroundings without producing specular images.

ANTHONY CARO (born 1924)

Caro was trained and works in England and was an assistant to Henry Moore from 1951–53. The merest glance at his sculptures (Plate 8, Figs 17 and 18) demonstrates their close relationship with those of Smith, who from 1959 was the primary influence upon him. Equally obvious is the decisive difference which is an almost complete absence of reference to the figure (or to Surrealism) and that this is associated with the prevailing horizontality of his sculpture. The support has been eliminated from the typical Smith configuration, so that the sculptures stand on and directly relate to the floor. For Caro: '. . . if you can make the floor act as part of the sculpture and not just [as a] base, the pieces will float' (Caro, 1972, p. 56).

The parts of Caro's sculptures do indeed float, they defy gravity. The effect is

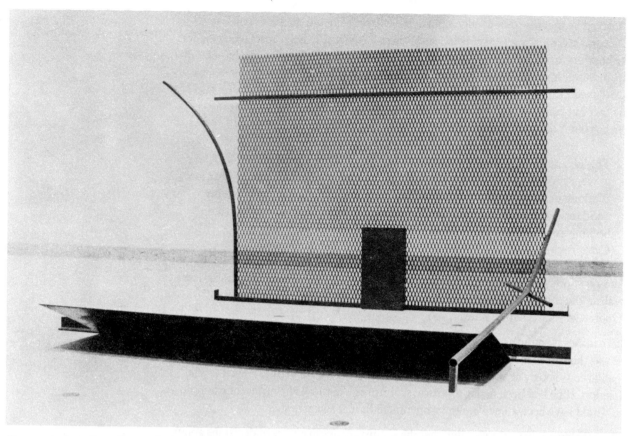

Figure 17 Anthony Caro, *Source*, mixed materials (Collection Museum of Modern Art, New York; photo: courtesy of the Robert Hunt Library).

Figure 18 Anthony Caro, *Table Piece XCVII*, 1970 (Kasmin Gallery, London; photo: John Goldblatt, courtesy of the Robert Hunt Library).

achieved by making joins at edges and ends, or by having unbalanced cantilevers. Caro works by placing elements in space; these have usually been abstract elements without the associations of the parts of Smith's sculpture, although Caro has bought up and used some of the older sculptor's unused stock. The relationship or syntax of Caro's sculptures is one of assemblage or, better, agglutination. The parts remain distinct but contribute to the meaning of the whole, which emerges only at the end. He has put it like this:

> The advantage of making them where I can't stand back from them was . . . to prevent my falling back on my previous knowledge of balance and composition. . . . Working in a one-car garage, as I used to do, was a way of trying to force my mind to accept a new kind of rightness that I wanted—I had to refrain from backing away and editing the work prematurely.
> (Caro, 1972, p. 56.)

And on another occasion: '. . . working . . . close up all the time my decisions don't bear on the thing's all round appearance; they're not compositional decisions.' (Quoted in Whitechapel Gallery, 1963.)

Caro makes it sound as if he gained from the accident of his work space but of course he was the heir to many artists who tried to avoid premature editing. It is more likely that he consciously or subconsciously worked on a large scale to put himself in that position. If he had been making vertical sculptures like those of Smith, for example, he would have been able to see the whole and edit it at an early stage.

Nevertheless we have the paradox that the sculptures are made up of decisions about relationships but are not 'compositional'. This disappears if you think of the relationships, whether in the making of the piece or the looking at it, as taking place in time or, more accurately, in succession, while 'composition' in sculpture implies a static balancing of one form against another. With an acute awareness of the limitations of the analogy he has said:

> I have been trying to eliminate references and make truly abstract sculpture, composing the parts of the pieces like notes in music. Just as a succession of these make up a melody or a sonata, so I take anonymous units and try to make them cohere in an open way into a sculptural whole. Like music, I would like my sculpture to be the expression of feeling in terms of the material, and, like music, I don't want the entirety of the experience to be given all at once.

This view appears to contradict what is said above of Rothko (p. 23). However there is an important distinction in that a sculpture, especially one of an open or dispersed configuration like those of Caro, presents a succession of dramatically changing shapes and relationships as you move round it, while a painting can only be looked at more or less from the front and seems much more constant. In the case of Caro, therefore, the passage of time and the full achievement of the experience of the sculpture can be marked (as in music) by a series of events or perceptions. In the case of Rothko time is marked only by a growth in the response of the viewer to a unitary experience.

From 1960 Caro has used paint, normally a single colour chosen after the structure was complete, to unify the sculpture and to reduce further the specific associations of the elements, including the apparent mass. The colour also emphasizes the visual rather than the tactile quality of his work and may sometimes give meaning to the title. However, from about 1966, many works have features which contradict the synthesis described above. For example, the *Table Piece* (Fig. 18) is on a base, it uses found elements which can be read, ploughshares, and it is composed like a picture. These features are clearly self-conscious and seem to be a means of testing the limits of his assumptions. Although on a base, like all the *Table Pieces*, XCVII hangs over the edge so it could not be on the ground. Although framed like a painting, the frame is at an angle to the real support, and the parts spill out beyond it. It is composed, but the twist of the shares makes it necessary to move around and explore the piece. Although smallish, its loose structure makes it difficult to imagine picking it up. It remains, therefore, visual rather than tactile.

One of Caro's closest associates has been the American painter, Kenneth Noland. Born in 1924, Noland worked in Washington up to 1961 and was a close friend of Morris Louis (see pp. 25–26); indeed it might be said that he was Louis's eyes and ears outside the studio. Noland visited New York frequently and reported what he found to the older artist. He was responsible specifically for the contact with the critic Clement Greenberg, which led to the visit to see the painting by Helen Frankenthaler that influenced both artists decisively. It is probable that the sight of the painting would not have had such an effect if they had not been directed to it mentally as well as physically by Greenberg. It would not be too much to say that this critic ,who had proved himself able to discern the best in the art of his day and to articulate his enthusiasm, on this occasion was able to indicate to these two artists both a technique and a direction associated with it, that they were to explore fruitfully but with very different results. The differences, of course, derive from the human differences of sensibility and experience.

Anthony Caro was also decisively influenced by meeting Greenberg. Another friend they shared in common was the writer Michael Fried, who has written consistently on both artists. Although I have quoted some remarks of Caro's I believe that the best way to understand these artists is to read what Greenberg, Fried and William Rubin have written about them (see the Recommended Reading list, p. 91). What they write, together with the intercommunication that forms the preparation for the writing, appears to feed back into the art that the painter and the sculptor have produced. Rather than attempt to describe or place Noland, therefore, I am going to leave it to Fried: see the Appendix, pp. 6–8, with Plate 9 and Figures 19 and 20.

Fried's (and Noland's) position derives from Greenberg (see Chipp, pp. 577–81). The Appendix (pp. 4–5) includes excerpts from another, later text which is more specific on the question of the integrity of the medium which is the backbone of this, the formalist tradition in art and criticism. A second quotation from Fried (Appendix, p. 6) reemphasizes that it is the great artists who determine what are to be the role and preoccupations of art. The whole synthesis descends substantially from Hans Hofmann, from whom Greenberg learned much. Here is an early remark by Greenberg (1939):

> Picasso, Braque, Mondrian, Miró, Kandinsky, Brancusi, even Klee, Matisse and Cézanne, derive their chief inspiration from the medium they work in. (Footnote: I owe this formulation to a remark made by Hans Hofmann . . .) The excitement of their art seems to lie most of all in its pure preoccupation with the invention and arrangement of spaces, surfaces, shapes, colors, etc., to *the exclusion of whatever is not necessarily implicated in these factors.*

A productive interrelation between artists and critics is certainly not new in art, but such relationships have been exceptionally important in the post-war New York School. The relationship of the Abstract Expressionists to certain critics, including Greenberg and Harold Rosenberg, was very strong.

Exercise

Compare the picture of Abstract Expressionism given by Rosenberg in the excerpts in the Appendix, pp. 8–9, with the formalist approach embodied in the Greenberg and Fried texts. (You may have noticed that the discussions of individual works in this unit generally follow a formalist method.) Reread Gleizes's and Metzinger's 'Cubism', Chipp, pp. 207 *ff.*, for another approach.

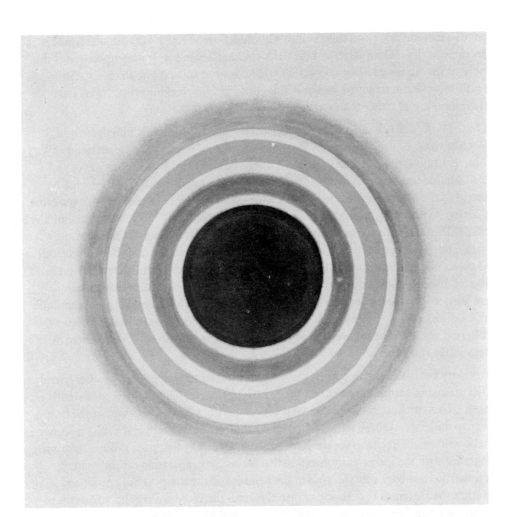

Figure 19 Kenneth Noland, *Spring Call*, 1961, oil, 82½ × 82½ ins (Private collection; photo: Rudolph Burckhardt, courtesy of Kenneth Noland and Andre Emmerich Gallery Inc.).

Figure 20 Kenneth Noland, *Up Cadmium*, 1965, acrylic resin paint on canvas, 72 × 216 ins point to point (Andre Emmerich Gallery, New York; photo: Rudolph Burckhardt).

Discussion

In reading Greenberg and Fried you may have been reminded of Gleizes's and Metzinger's 'Cubism', especially section I leading up to the penultimate paragraph on p. 209. They argue that modernist art is validated by a pedigree of great artists, each building on and reacting to what went immediately before. The progression from Courbet's 'realistic impulse' to Cézanne's 'painting is not, or is no longer, the art of imitating an object by means of lines and colours but the art of giving our instinct a plastic consciousness'. Both the writers of 1912 and those of the 1960s describe a dialectic process of history (though not a Marxist one) and seem to imply that only an artist who goes along with history has any chance of being great. In effect, a problem in criticism is set to each generation by the previous one. In our era it takes the form 'what remains at this moment that cannot be eliminated'. However, Greenberg is careful not to assert that this is a law, only that the best artists have followed such a path. For Rosenberg, everything in life is relevant *but* criticism. The painting is a crucial action in the individual *life* of the artist. It is not an event in art, still less in art history, which the artist has 'sent to the devil'.

Rosenberg's view was closer to the statements of the artists he was writing about and it is applicable to many others—Rauschenberg, Warhol, the Conceptual artists. It represents the ambition of freedom and responsibility central to western art. However, it is too ambitious. A study of the work of most of the best artists shows that they do indeed appear to fix on issues set by their immediate predecessors, and are pre-occupied by the medium in which they work, as this whole course demonstrates. There are certain exceptions, but even a very great artist cannot altogether transcend his age and, no matter how exceptional his work, the value given to his achievement will always attract both imitators and those who will be fascinated by and try to go beyond what he has done. Art is an activity defined by its practitioners so there can be no other course.

Both Greenberg and Rosenberg speak of eliminating what is not necessary. Both see this process as a way of making room for what is important either at the moment in history or to the artist personally. Such a process seems to me absolutely essential and has its analogues in political and scientific development. However, I think Greenberg's identification of it with the tendency to ever greater respect for the flatness of the canvas is too limiting, even though that tendency has been both recurrent and fruitful in the period under consideration.

Assemblage and Neo-Dada

This section, although it includes some of the finest post-war artists, may be thought of as transitional between Abstract Expressionism and the emergence of Pop and certain kinds of Conceptual Art.

The term 'Assemblage' emphasizes the aspect of the inclusion of ready-made, usually used, or 'junk' objects, in paintings and sculpture. 'Neo-Dada' refers to the aspect of the questioning of the notion of art, usually through the means of presenting for aesthetic response objects, events and ideas which had not traditionally been considered within the frame of reference of art. The influence of Duchamp has clearly been very strong. A long quotation in Chipp, pp. 606–16, presents the point of view of one of the pioneers of 'Assemblage', Dubuffet.

JASPER JOHNS (born 1930)

Like Rauschenberg (see p. 37) Johns's art came to a maturity soon after Abstract Expressionism and can be seen both as a continuation of it and as a reaction to it or to the theories of art associated with it (Plate 10 and Haftmann 995 and 996).
In the illustrations the differences from Abstract Expressionism are much more obvious than the likenesses. The most obvious difference is the presence of a commonplace object, literally represented; in every case, however, the thing represented is itself an image and itself flat. By a kind of sleight of hand, Johns has reintroduced the associations of the subject without resorting to creating an illusion, and has reintroduced meaning without having to invent an image or even to reveal himself at all.

In his paintings, there is no clue to his attitude to the numbers or to the flags. At first glance they reveal none of the passion or the ambition to go deep into the human condition that those of Pollock or Newman did—instead there is an apparent banality. Looking more closely you see that the pictures are elaborately worked. They are as painterly as those of Still or de Kooning, but the brush strokes (Johns used the ancient technique of encaustic, or painting in melted wax) are free only within the limits of the conventional pattern of his adopted image.

Now read the excerpts from the interviews with David Sylvester and Gene Swenson and from the essay by John Cage (Appendix, pp. 9–11). They show a kind of thought and attitude very different from that of, say, Still or Rothko: elusive but precise, quiet but obsessive. The question is not one of representation or of expression but of existence and meaning: Swenson: 'But shouldn't the artist have an attitude to his subject, shouldn't he transform it?' Johns: 'Transformation is in the head. If you have one thing and make another thing, there is no transformation, but there are two things. I don't think you would mistake one for another.' Johns explains to Sylvester that what we see as a thing depends on our mental set at the moment and Cage gives an instance in his story of the woman who changed her mind about the *Beer Cans*. By *re*composing the flag in paint rather than painting a picture of a flag in the world (How often do you see a real flag standing out perfectly flat?) Johns raises the issue of what is seen as a flag. It is necessary for him to use a very familiar image in order to get this effect. It is also necessary for this to be an image from outside 'high art' because the conversion 'non-art' to 'art' is parallel to and associated with the conversion 'bunting' to 'paint on canvas' and must be noticed by the viewer.

Where Johns represents a three-dimensional object he represents it in three dimensions but changes the materials and the details of surface. The scale is not changed, for the scale of, for example, a torch, is part of its use and therefore, as he says, its meaning. There is literally an exception which proves this rule in the *Beer Cans*. One of these is slightly larger than the other but either, taken alone, would seem the right size. The flat images that he uses, being images, have no intrinsic scale. How big is the number five (Haftmann 995)? You can compare this painting with a painting which was very well known, by Demuth (Haftmann 817—*I saw the Figure 5 in Gold*) and the latter with Johns' *Three Flags*, Plate 10. Demuth's figures recede in an illusion of space as if they were real objects depicted; Johns' flags are mental objects built up in real space. This picture also makes clear the meaning of the quotation above about transformation. It is important here that the image and the canvases are conterminous —there is no field of canvas around the flag. Seeing this, one can read again Haftmann 996 and see that the orange field is as much part of the object which is the painting as the flag is, that it is no more an object in space than the stars on a blue field in the flag itself. (The term 'field' is used in describing flags.)

ROBERT RAUSCHENBERG (born 1925)

> Painting relates to both art and life. Neither can be made. I try to act in the gap between the two.

This remark by Rauschenberg must be one of the most quoted in the history of recent art. On this occasion, however, I want to try to illuminate the statement by citing paintings and other works of art; to reverse the usual process of illuminating the painting by a statement. However such a statement is, of course, itself a work of art.

Nude Blueprint, c. 1949. This was made by lying a woman on light-sensitive blueprint paper so that, when processed, the imprint of her body appeared on it.

Tyre Print, 1951. Rauschenberg's description:

> I did a twenty-foot print and John Cage was involved in this because he was the only person with a car who would be willing to do this. I glued together fifty [actually twenty] sheets of paper—the largest I had— and stretched it out on the street. He drove his A-model Ford through the paint and onto the paper. He did a beautiful job and I consider it my print.

(Cage taught at Black Mountain College where Rauschenberg had gone to acquire a discipline. He is the composer of a piece for piano in which the pianist sits silent for exactly four minutes thirty-three seconds and the music is the noises made by the audience or those that penetrate the hall from outside; he has also influenced many younger artists.) Cage himself wrote:

> Is when Rauschenberg looks an idea? Rather it is an entertainment to celebrate unfixity. . . . I know he put the paint on the tyres. And he unrolled the paper on the city street. But which one of us drove the car?

In 1952 Rauschenberg produced some all-white paintings:

> I always thought of the white paintings as being not passive, but very—well hyper-sensitive, so that one could look at them and almost see how many people were in the room by the shadows cast, or what time of day it was.

This acceptance of accident may be related in a close way to the abjuration of conscious control practised more or less completely by the Surrealists and Abstract Expressionists. However, what replaces it is not the unconscious but events in the 'world'.

> I'm opposed to the whole idea of conception-execution—of getting an idea for a picture and then carrying it out. I've always felt as though whatever I've used and whatever I've done, the method was always closer to a *collaboration* with materials than to any kind of conscious manipulation and control.

37

In 1953 he erased a drawing by de Kooning (with the artist's consent). De Kooning had just reached the height of his reputation and the gesture was certainly meant to be shocking, but it also asserts that a work of art can be a destruction as well as a construction. Indeed it always is. The drawing destroys the white paper, the (renewed) white paper, the drawing. Both acts are those of artists.

Rauschenberg's mature work, beginning in about 1954, is less obviously extreme than this (Haftmann 993 and 994, Plate 11). These works are a mixture of paint (art) and objects (life) but 'I was so involved with the materials separately, that I didn't want painting to be simply an act of employing one color to do something to another color'. He painted all black or all white and he bought tins of paint that had lost their labels so that he would not know what colour he was about to use until he began to put it on. Such a gesture implies that paint is a material not a colour. *Bed* (Plate 11) shows him acting directly on life with paint, but the result is art or life according to the prejudice of the viewer (see quote in the Appendix, pp. 11–12). He describes these pictures as 'combine paintings'. They include objects either on or in (literally) the canvas as the bottles are 'in' *Curfew* (Haftmann 993) or objects are painted. The objects may include sound (whatever programme is picked-up by a radio attached to the picture) or growing grass (see Hans Haacke, p. 82). Many include illustrations from papers or magazines but from 1963 he started incorporating images by means of photo-silk-screen printing. Although the material is paint, these images replace the objects as 'life' in the paintings; they are combined freely and allusively—as in *Tracer* (Haftmann 994).

JEAN TINGUELY (born 1925)

Tinguely is best known as the maker of elaborate and ungainly, but charming, machines that move in an erratic and absurd manner, constantly breaking down. His teacher in Switzerland (where he was born) was very interested in the *Merzbau* of Schwitters (see Unit 13) and encouraged students to work with any kind of material that came to hand; the influence of Klee is also obvious in Tinguely's work. He believes in the principle of the universality of movement but thinks of it not in the terms of simple rotations and velocities (like Gabo, for instance) but in terms of the interaction of so many forces that the result, like life, is quite unpredictable. That his machines break down or destroy themselves is an essential part of them, for otherwise the movement would become too predictable, that is, in effect, static. Such a concept of art is consciously or unconsciously a criticism of the idea of a work of art as the permanent (collectable) manifestation of the genius of the artist and is a forerunner of the performance and disposable art of the next generation.

One of Tinguely's most celebrated creations, *Homage to New York* (Fig. 21), was a huge machine, set up in the courtyard of the Museum of Modern Art, New York, that was intended to set off fireworks and spray the smart audience with water, while smashing itself to pieces. In the event, it failed to destroy itself, but caught fire and had to be destroyed by the New York Fire Department, a result that delighted the artist, for it clearly involved an extra force, that of the city officials.

A whole series of machines includes violently oscillating arms to which spectators can attach crayons or felt-pens which move over paper and produce in seconds parodies of Abstract Expressionist painting. Tinguely was pleased that such a machine was excluded from an exhibition by other artists because it was not safe; he set it up outside where it attracted most of the attention. (An account of another occasion is given in the Appendix, p. 12.)

Although all three of these artists are primarily makers of objects, it is clear from their activities and statements that they regard the function of art, at its most general, as being the changing of consciousness. The works of art are not pictures of particular objects or scenes, but are nevertheless pictures of the world: representations of certain characteristics of the world, above all, of the fact that perception of it is conditioned by human conventions and expectations.

Figure 21 Jean Tinguely, *Homage to New York*, a self-constructing and destroying work of art, demonstration in the Sculpture Garden of the Museum of Modern Art, New York, 17 March 1960 (Photo: David Gahr).

Exercise

Do you see any analogy between the development of the art of these three artists and Greenberg's account of the development of Modernism?

Discussion

Both traditions are concerned with stripping art of its unnecessary conventions as soon as these are seen to be unnecessary and with the integrity of the medium left after the stripping has taken place. The difference is that the medium is defined in one case with reference to materials, paint and canvas, and in the other with reference to the functional role of art. The art of Tinguely, Rauschenberg and Johns (together with many others, some of whom are discussed later) asserts that art can be made out of anything, whether material or mental; the convention to be discarded is that of the physical medium. There is a strong tendency for art of this kind (see again the Futurists, Russian Cubo-Futurists and Dadaists) to become events. What cannot be discarded is the concept of art itself; this is defined practically as what the artist does —'if the artist says it is art, it is art' and 'who is the artist?'; 'the one who makes art'. This position is not tautologous if 'art' and 'artist' are understood in terms of roles, constantly evolving in a continuous manner. Art, as in Greenberg's view, is based on what went before, what great artists have done, and is a comment on that. But art is also thought of as symbolic; the work of art is symbolic and the role of artist in society is symbolic so that what the artist does is always seen as a comment on 'life'. However it is a comment on life which is to be seen as part of life and not one standing outside life. Greenberg's stressing the physicality, the flatness of the picture and Rauschenberg's acting in the gap between life and art are both statements of this view.

39

Happenings

(This art form is dealt with by Paul Overy in TV programme 10, *Art as Performance*.)

Before the name 'Happenings' gained more general use, Allan Kaprow, one of the initiators, referred to them as 'Action Collages'. This was not a bad term. It was applied to a number of contrived occasions having the character of collage in that each was made up of a sequence of events, including people and objects, that existed in real time and space but did not have the coherent narrative character or illusory time of a theatre performance. The people in them did not play roles although their actions were largely controlled by a scenario. The audience was not separated from the action but often participated at least to the extent of moving around; such a device reinforces the apparent reality of the events and prevents them from acquiring the character of an illusion or simulation. The effect of the Happening derives from the juxtaposition of events, but the structure of the whole is not only untheatrical, it is also unlike real-life situations, such as work or the family, where elaborated conventions allow us to make sense of the most unexpected events. In a Happening the events may be commonplace or shocking individually, but the relationship between them, as between the elements of a collage, resists rationalization.

YVES KLEIN (1928–62)

Some of the activities of Rauschenberg recall not only those of Duchamp but of a French contemporary, Klein, one of the most influential artists in Europe during the late fifties and sixties. TV programme 10, *Art as Performance*, shows film of Klein causing naked girls to spread paint on their bodies and, under his direction, to press or move against the canvas so as to produce a painting. The emphasis in these works, the *Anthropométries* (Fig. 22), is on the process of making them, presented as a ritual. Klein always wore evening clothes, like the conductor of an orchestra, and performed in front of a 'first-night' audience. In principle, however, they are only part of a wider range of paintings made by imprinting natural events onto canvases. They derive from Dubuffet and from Abstract Expressionism, and I shall describe here some more prophetic enterprises.

In 1947 Klein conceived the idea of doing paintings in a single colour (later called *Monochromes*) and composed a symphony of a single extended note. Later he exhibited such paintings, first in a variety of colours and then (in 1957) all in a single special blue paint which he patented as 'International Klein Blue'. He used the same blue on a variety of other objects. In 1958 his exhibition at the Galérie Iris Clert, in Paris, consisted of the completely bare interior of the gallery painted white and the exterior painted blue, guarded by two uniformed members of the Garde Républicaine (the French President's Guards). The exhibition was a *succès de scandale* (see Unit 1, Fig. 7). The importance of this work, called *Le Vide*, is the assertion that the artist can take possession of (and sell) a certain aesthetic experience, in the way that a landscape painter takes possession of a view, but without converting it into a work of art. It uses commercial and official systems to make the point. Klein devised an even more complete assertion of the same concept in 1957–59 which was carried out in 1960–62. This was the sale of seven 'Zones of Pictorial Sensibility', which were numbered but unspecified, for a quantity of gold leaf. The purchaser of each was given a receipt but only took 'possession' of the 'Zone' when he had destroyed the receipt and when the artist had thrown away half of the gold leaf.

As the role he played in the *Anthropométries* demonstrates, Klein was a part of his own art works, as the Italian and Russian Futurists as well as Dada and Surrealist artists had been on occasions. One work (1960), intended to demonstrate his possession of

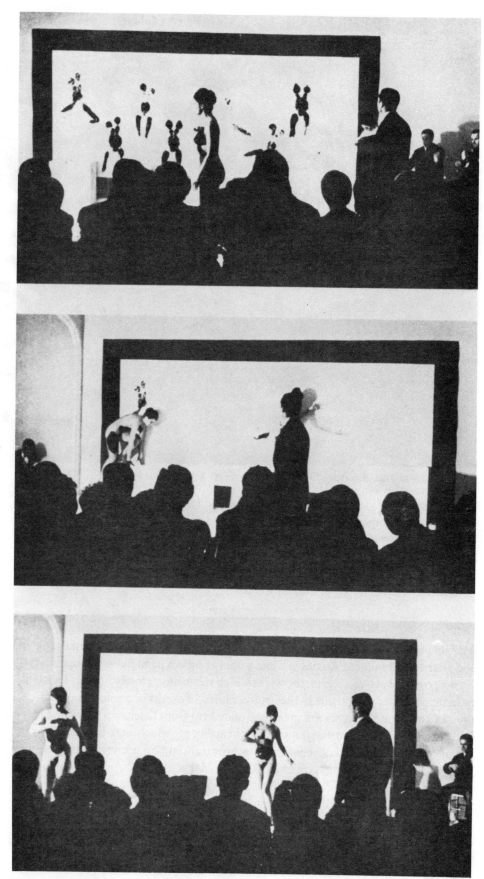

Figure 22 first public exhibition of *Anthropométries*, Paris, March 1960 (Courtesy of Mme Klein Moquay, Galerie Karl Flinker, Paris © ADAGP Paris 1976).

'space', involved his diving to the ground from the level of a first-floor window in order to be photographed in flight (Fig. 23); his advanced judo training limited his injuries. Although this work was located in the first place entirely in his person, from

Figure 23 Klein in Space (Courtesy of Mme Klein Moquay © ADAGP Paris 1976).

the public point of view it took the form of a reproduced photograph. This also is an allegory of the complete autonomy of the artist and of the purely documentary role assigned to the art work (for further examples of this position, see pp. 72*ff.*). Klein's attitude as expressed both in his writings and in his work is romantic and artistocratic but the artists he influenced, or at least those whose work shares the same direction, have been overwhelmingly of the political left.

PIERO MANZONI (1933–63)

Manzoni saw the first exhibition of Klein's uniform blue paintings in Milan in 1957 and afterwards produced a series of white works using not paint but white materials— plaster, cotton wool, etc. Again, the works which relate most closely to what I shall be describing in later sections are in the nature, rather, of events or ironic demonstrations of aspects of the art system in the line of descent from Duchamp's *Urinal*. He sold copies of his thumb print, put some of them on eggs which were to be eaten by visitors to the exhibition, balloons full of his breath and tins of preserved 'artist's shit'. He signed people, declaring them to be works by Manzoni (Fig. 24) and inscribed a cube with the words '*Socle du monde*' ('Base of the world') which he turned upside down so that the earth could be thought of as standing upon it and becoming his sculpture. Some of his pieces have a deliberate catch in them that parodies the tradition of the art market. He sold lines of various lengths for proportionate sums of money but in certain cases the line was buried, or the owner was prevented in other ways from being able to check whether he had got true 'value for money'. But, of course, in an art context, he would not need to know; the value of a work of art is imagined to be related only to its quality not to its size. All of these works present 'the thing as it is' with the intention of asserting that it has great power without the artist intervening to rearrange or dramatize it. Some of them emphasize the quality of sheer physicality in the most intimate form of the bodies of people and their secretions.

NOUVEAU RÉALISME

Tinguely and Yves Klein can also be ascribed to the *Nouveau Réalisme* movement, but the latter also contained a Pop element (see p. 46). I give only one example (Fig. 25) a *décollage* by Mimmo Rotella. Several artists made *décollages* reversing the usual process of collage: they began with superimposed posters and created an art work by tearing strips off them. Pierre Restany, the spokesman of the movement, argued that all styles were exhausted and that reality would be put in their place (Manifesto, Milan, 1961) and that

> The New Realists consider the world as a picture, the great fundamental masterpiece from which they take fragments endowed with universal significance. . . . And through these specific images the whole social reality, the common wealth of human activity is brought before us.

The tone of this and of many of the art works it supported is much more rhetorical than contemporary British or American writing; the political element is more explicit. The purpose of the paintings is to reveal social reality, as it is symbolized by typical products of industrial society, especially posters, magazines, etc., in which sophisticated men try to make large numbers of people buy their goods by associating them

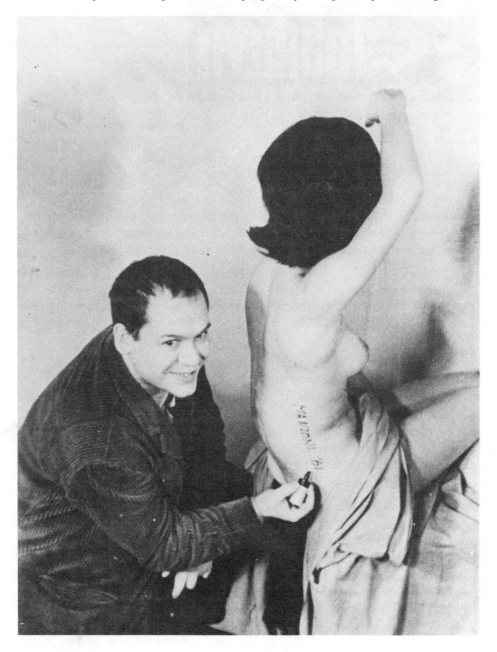

Figure 24 Piero Manzoni signing a woman (Germano Celant, Genoa).

43

Figure 25 Mimmo Rotella, *Marilyn Monroe*, 1962, collage (Collection Fritz and Agnes Becht, Hilversum; photo: Studio Hartland).

with an imagery and ideology of the good life. *Nouveau Réalisme* modulated contrived, real-life events and is part of the prehistory of the event or performance art of the present day in which social comment can be much more trenchant.

Exercise

What do you think is the role of the erotic or 'shocking' features of Klein and Manzoni's art?

Discussion

Both the use of nude models (nearly all female) in Klein's *Anthropométries* and the signing of nude models as works of art by Manzoni are directly related to the tradition of the nude in art, which is thousands of years old. You cannot include a woman in a painting in the way that you can include a newspaper in a collage, but you can imprint her on the canvas and you can turn her into a sculpture by signing her. This can be seen to correspond to the Greek myth of Pygmalion and Galataea—the sculpture which came to life.

There is an almost equally old association of artists with sexual freedom—one of the cornerstones of the myth of the bohemian. Both these artists are certainly playing up to this. They are also playing up to the idea of *épater le bourgeois* (shocking the middle classes) but at the same time, making the middle classes like it. The throwing away of gold and the tins of 'artist's shit' are examples of the same activity. Both are in part a comment on the fact that, since the triumph of the Impressionists, no matter what the artist does, there is a collector who will buy. Most people would regard a person's faeces as the most noxious thing he can produce—if a collector will buy that, he will indeed buy anything. Manzoni offered tins of 'artist's shit' for sale, but who will open one to see if it really contains what the label says? Perhaps it is just a tin of food, not noxious at all. This is the idea of the 'Emperor's New Clothes' in reverse. But also, faeces are the only 'sculpture', that is solid objects, produced by the body involuntarily and by the mere act of living. Is this a comment on automatism? Even the most automatic painting requires the artist to obey the conventions of paint and canvas and is therefore not altogether unconscious.

Pop in Britain

Lawrence Alloway first used the term 'Pop Art' to mean popular commercial art and design on the analogy of the much older 'pop music' but it came to mean fine art or high art which draws imagery from such commercial-art, or low-art, sources. There were separate but roughly simultaneous movements in Britain and America; they have in common the use of imagery, mostly drawn from American culture, but they are very different both in their attitudes to the material and stylistically and formally (compare Figs 25–33, Plates 12–16).

Before trying to particularize the differences I must distinguish these kinds of Pop from Realism, although one of the contemporary terms for it was 'New Realism' following the French *Nouveau Réalisme*. Almost every kind of twentieth-century art has been called realist. It can mean representational or abstract ('the picture is real'); it can mean merely that the subject is important or that the style proposes a 'higher' reality than the physical, like the fourth dimension. None of these meanings is relevant to Pop and I take 'Realism' to mean an art that represents and emphasizes the *physical* substance of things, including people, as the art of Courbet (see Unit 1) does. If Pop Art asserts the reality of anything it is the reality of the chosen image, not that of the object represented by the image.

In England the origins of Pop can be found in a series of lectures and discussions organized at the Institute of Contemporary Arts (ICA) by the Independent Group (IG) between 1952 and 1955. The IG included architects, designers, scientists, technologists, art historians, critics and other professionals as well as artists. Its earlier sessions were often intended to confront art specialists with imagery and thought systems, especially scientific, that were outside their own tradition. In this it had early heroes and precedents in Amédée Ozenfant's *The Foundations of Modern Art* (1928; see Unit 6) and the biologist D'Arcy Thompson's *Growth and Form*; these books treated the design of industrial and natural objects with the aesthetic awareness usually applied to fine art. But, almost from the first, it was clear that many members shared an interest in another imagery that was closer to, but still outside, fine art—one that was more completely despised by the art establishment.

At the second meeting the sculptor Eduardo Paolozzi, who had always preferred science and ethnographic museums to art museums, projected onto the screen in succession, a series of images in which machines were mixed with covers of science-fiction and confession magazines, pin-ups, film publicity, packaging, advertising, photo-journalism: almost the whole gamut of the visual consumption of contemporary urban cultures. A commentary was given on some of these items by Reyner Banham who later gave a talk in which he analysed the iconography of contemporary motorcar design, treating it with the same method and respect that, as an Art historian, he had learned to give to the paintings of the Renaissance. The message was that both in the making and in the consumption of the commercial arts there existed degrees of skill and sensibility that were the equal of those that could be found in the high arts. That is, as Lawrence Alloway put it, there was a 'Pop-Fine Art continuum', rather than a pyramid with fine art at the top and Pop at the bottom. This was also a political message since the subcultures embodying these skills were essentially working and lower middle class. Semantics and semiotics (the sciences of signs and signification) were much discussed, also sociological and anthropological accounts of language and culture in both urban and primitive societies. The discussion of automobile styling mentioned above and a lecture by Lawrence Alloway on violence in the movies (the preferred term for films) were essentially semantic exercises but reflected a respect for, even a pride in, the material. This is very different from the European approach which has tended to see popular commercial culture as a means of oppressing the working classes.

46

Paolozzi himself did not at this time produce Pop art; he subjected his material to complex metamorphoses (see Chipp, pp. 616 ff.) and it was only later that he exhibited the images of his lecture under the title *Bunk*. Accordingly the credit for producing the first truly Pop work of art is usually given to Richard Hamilton for his *Just What is it Makes Today's Homes So Different, So Appealing?* (Plate 12). This collage was printed in silk screen as the poster for an exhibition called 'This is Tomorrow' (Whitechapel Gallery, London, 1956). It contains references to most of the fields I have mentioned. The sky is an image of space; there are male and female pin-ups, television, pulp romance, consumer durables, packaging, the movies in the headless but nevertheless instantly recognizable figure of Al Jolson, automobile heraldry and even the word 'Pop'.

A finer and more characteristic work of Hamilton's is *Hommage à Chrysler Corp.* (Plate 13). Here the title's fusion of French and American words and cultural stereotypes is mirrored in the combination of a Cézannesque style with references to the kind of automobile motifs described by Reyner Banham in his lecture. The spiral drawing just above the centre is a piece of human style-engineering—a bra. Hamilton was very conscious that the information given by commercial imagery was not merely a matter of iconography but of graphic devices appropriate to that iconography. A visually literate consumer would be aware of or at least respond to this factor. *Hommage à Chrysler Corp.* is as much an anthology of styles or means of representation as a compendium of references. There are, for example, several different conventions for representing chrome—high-art and low-art brush-work (one showing the artist's hand, the other anonymous), hard and soft focus, line and half-tone, etc. (see Hamilton's description in the Appendix, pp. 12–13). The concern with medium understood in these terms (which are of course far removed from Hofmann's notion of medium) is common to several of the younger generation of British artists who have been associated with Pop.

The Independent Group was the most important starting point for British Pop. A second was the work of Francis Bacon. Bacon was at the time the one older painter in this country who received virtually universal respect from the younger artists and students. Haftmann reproduces two paintings of 1945: 948 and 949; these exemplify the sense of godless futility, of man as meat, that is implied by certain phrases in the texts quoted by Chipp, pp. 920–22. These selections also bring out the fact that he sees painting not as a means of representation, however 'distorted', but as a struggle to invent means of recreating experience: they dwell on the importance of his use of existing images. These may be photographs or paintings—he has used images from films, the head of the woman with broken glasses, a frequently published still from the Odessa steps sequence of Eisenstein's *Battleship Potemkin*, X-ray photographs and other medical illustrations, images from Muybridge's photographs of men and animals in motion and, in the example illustrated, Velasquez's portrait of Pope Innocent X (Fig. 26). This picture shows Bacon using several different kinds of notation or representational convention in one painting and also that the surfaces of objects are discontinuous so that the figure appears to be a kind of hallucination. This characteristic occurs in several of the Pop painters but without any of the suggestion of anxiety that it has in Bacon.

A third and still more distant part of the ground from which Pop emerged was the so-called 'kitchen-sink' school (John Bratby, Jack Smith, Edward Middleditch and others), associated with the Royal College of Art. It was an anti-aesthetic and anti-establishment movement characterized by large pictures of commonplace domestic subjects painted in a deliberately coarse manner. Although the group was publicized as a school of social realism, the paintings were as likely to contain cornflake packets and other brand goods as the more usual subject matter of social realist art.

The younger generation of Pop artists appeared in two waves, also at the Royal College of Art: the first in the middle and late fifties included Richard Smith, Joe

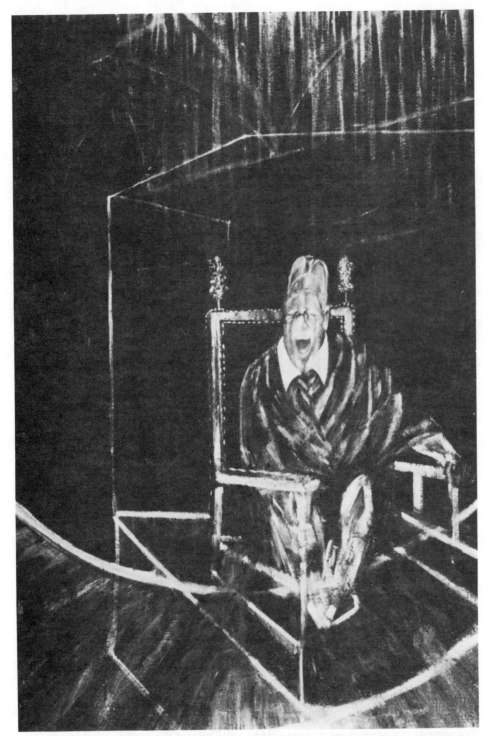

Figure 26 Francis Bacon, *Pope II*, 1951, oil, 78 × 54 ins (Kunsthalle, Mannheim; photo: courtesy of the Marlborough Gallery, London).

Tilson and Peter Blake; the second, in 1959–62, Ronald Kitaj, David Hockney, Patrick Caulfield, Derek Boshier, Allen Jones and Peter Phillips. Most of these exhibited at the 'Young Contemporaries', an annual exhibition of student work, and it was there in 1961 and 1962 that Pop Art achieved an instant fame and critical recognition which led to exhibitions in dealer's galleries and museums. However of all these artists only Peter Phillips has consistently produced work which can be regarded as firmly within the Pop canon.

The generation of Smith and Tilson reacted against or ignored the kitchen-sink trend. Sharing the same antipathy to the art of the high culture they did not accept the formal banality and crude approach to the problem of representation. They inherited sophisticated awareness of the urban media from the IG and from their reading, but they were also the generation that emerged from art school at the moment of the two great exhibitions of American art in London which revealed the powerful achievement of the Abstract Expressionists. A fusion of these two resources can be found in abstract artists like Robyn Denny and Bernard Cohen, but Smith is more relevant to the present context.

RICHARD SMITH (born 1931)

Most of Smith's painting is abstract and executed with a painterly handling which relates it to Abstract Expressionism. However, always, and most obviously in the early sixties, it reflects his interest in the qualities of advertisements and packaging, particularly those that express an ideal of luxurious living (see Appendix, pp. 13–14). His paintings often emulated the soft-focus effects, the preference for secondary colours like orange, pink or turquoise, and the repetitive shapes and sharp foreshortenings that were so characteristic of the advertisements in the up-market magazines. Plate 14 demonstrates that these were not treated literally but allusively like the landscape of figure in the work of other abstract artists. His sense of the paradox involved in applying, as paint to canvas, colours which derive from those produced by commercial reprographic processes seems to have led him to force the issue by painting on three-dimensional, shaped or warped surfaces. Some of these recall those large advertisements, often seen on the approaches to airports, where a painted three-dimensional image projects from a two-dimensional background. The sophisticated, allusive titles of his paintings are a key to the character of his use of 'pop' material: *Kent* (cigarettes), *Lubitsch*, *Fool's Blue*—all in the 1960s. Such titles are common to this generation of painters, including some of those whose work was most rigorously abstract, like Denny; it seems to derive from Hamilton but also more distantly from Duchamp. This is no coincidence, for not only is Hamilton one of the most serious students of the work of Duchamp, but he and most of the Pop artists share the older artist's concern to emphasize that painting is a mental act taking place in a complex cultural context. The title can be a means of indicating the ramifications of that context.

PETER BLAKE (born 1932)

Blake represents the opposite pole of Pop to Smith; his art seems to rest on an obsessive collector's love of the detritus of urban life: toys, post-cards, pin-ups, badges, flags. Much of this comes not from the highly sophisticated Madison Avenue or Hollywood 'Pop' culture but from the much more naive low-budget British popular culture. (The distinction was first made by Lawrence Alloway.) When Blake left the Royal College he got a grant to study such material, which has since become a modish staple of Portobello Road and 'antique' shops all over the world. (It is worth mentioning that several of the Pop artists lived, as students or soon after, in the area immediately adjacent to Portobello Road, which was just beginning to emerge as the junk metropolis of London.) Blake's paintings were encrusted with the same material, collaged on, or rendered literally. He was beginning to acquire a technique of exceptional refinement which could imitate not only the style, but the accidental minutiae of a medium and of wear and tear. Although the result may be highly illusionistic, the illusion is that of a familiar but at the same time unreal world, a fantasy that includes fairies, all-in wrestlers and the Beatles. The fantasy is always in the appropriate style and medium. The technique is like that of a picture restorer or faker, conjuring up the complete surface of a painting from a different time and place. Even the most recent material always seems slightly remote, as if it had belonged to someone else. Many of his pictures have been portraits of imaginary characters and are fitted out with little objects (see Fig. 27) which reflect the supposed tastes of this character: another kind of realism by association.

49

Figure 27 Peter Blake, *Doktor K. Tortur*, 1965, Kryla and collage on hardboard, 24 × 10 ins (Private collection; photo: courtesy of the Waddington Gallery, London).

DAVID HOCKNEY (born 1937)

Hockney's earlier work, like that of Blake, presents a world of his own personal likes and fantasies in a naive style. He is also, like Blake, an extremely skilful painter and draughtsman, a master of a wide range of styles; however, his world is much nearer the art world, and the world of sophisticated high life. His work contains references to objects in the Louvre and British Museum and portraits of intellectuals, rich and perceptive Los Angeles collectors (with some of their contemporary art) as well as references to Hollywood movies and images from body magazines. Some paintings of the early sixties imitated, or rather parodied in a friendly way, Cubist and other modernist styles; the more recent paintings have appeared to be more simply naturalistic, hiding formal and stylistic invention below the surface. They increasingly represent a real world, but one which is separated from that of most of us, by its own internal sense of style. It is just this attention to conscious and quoted style as a medium of expression that allies his art to Pop. I mean by this that we normally think of style as being an intrinsic, almost involuntary, part of a painting or sculpture, by representing the world in a certain way (abstract or naturalistic) the painter communicates his view of it; but Pop artists characteristically use style as if it were a given thing, a subject matter, as objective as other physical or mental objects.

The portrait of Isherwood and Bachardy (Plate 15) is a characteristic picture about style, while remaining a faithful and moving likeness of its sitters. The louvred shutters at the back, the neat piles of books and the symmetrically and orthogonally placed arm chairs, remind one inevitably of the contemporary abstract painting and sculpture; they are stylistic quotations like the more obvious quotations of Cubism and Abstract Expressionism that you find in earlier works. But the sparseness of the interior, the sense of coolness in a hot climate, and the relationship between the

Figure 28 Peter Phillips, *Custom Painting No. 2*, 1964, oil, 84 × 69 ins (Private collection, New York; photo: courtesy of the artist).

sitters, which is one of acute mutual awareness, coupled with a distance which is not merely physical, all speak of a way of life imbued with style.

PETER PHILLIPS (born 1939)

Peter Phillips represents Pop at its sharpest focus in Britain. Read the quotation in the Appendix, pp. 14–15; Phillips says he has lived with his images as long as he can remember 'and so it's natural to use them without thinking'. Such images are again units that combine motifs with a characteristic style. Figure 28 includes technological diagrams, contemporary heraldry, and two kinds of high shine: a car advertisement and a pin-up. The images are related to each other, all expressing explosive power. The word 'custom' in the title refers to the 'customizing' of cars—the special paint jobs and the addition of attachments that give an air of extra performance to a regular model. Most of such additions do not affect positively the actual performance of the car, but they work by evoking an association with racing cars, aeroplanes, rockets and the effects of drugs. This is a painting that is entirely made up of such emblems. However Phillips seems to assert that they are so universal among his generation that they can be made the basis of an original statement just as the words and syntax of a shared language can be.

Pop in America

In the United States, Pop Art grew out of a quite different background to the movement in Britain. In the USA the most pervasive and conspicuous commercial culture was indigenous; it was not endowed with an exotic glamour or seen as an external threat to the native culture, and there was the strength of the current art and of the critical tradition that supported it.

Equally important was the economic state of art and of its institutions. By about 1953, American collectors, the richest and most acquisitive in the world, were convinced of the importance of their own school and in increasing numbers, turned from the School of Paris to the Abstract Expressionists. Dealers and critics were keen to discover new talent or new movements and to publicize them. There was, of course, an element of patriotism in this, or even chauvinism, which was officially supported by the circulation abroad of Abstract Expressionist paintings. The artists who had, in some cases, sought consciously to achieve a democratic art found themselves unexpectedly the representatives of market-economy democracy in the cold war. (This is not to say, of course, that there did not remain a much larger group hostile to the same art.) The Museum of Modern Art in New York, which had since 1928 built itself up into the most comprehensive and best selected collection of European art since the Impressionists, also began to collect contemporary American art more rapidly, in competition with the Whitney, a purely national museum, and to mount exhibitions which seemed to pick out and define new trends. Even the Metropolitan (equivalent to our National Gallery and British Museum) moved into the same field. Art history came up to date. Dealers, collectors, critics, historians and museum curators were all in a position to make their careers, like the artists themselves, out of the forward march of art. They were supported by a tax system that encouraged donations to museums. There was an especial advantage for donors of contemporary art in this, if they could get in quickly, for the system allowed them to purchase cheaply but to get tax exemption at the current assessed value, which could soon be very much more. That value could be positively affected by the acceptance of works by a major museum, still more by a large exhibition. Rauschenberg and Johns had great museum retrospectives aged 38 and 34, while de Kooning waited until 64 and Pollock died too soon at 44.

Pop Art, when it emerged, was a godsend to this industry, taking over when the market for the lesser Abstract Expressionists collapsed in the early 1960s, but I should say right away, that although the artists could hardly be unaware of the fact after a very short time, their art has remained astonishingly uncorrupted by it. It is as if, having taken commercial art as a starting point, they have been inoculated against the ravages of commercialism. Warhol is a special case in this respect, as I will try to show later. Pop had first of all the advantage of being instantly recognizable and memorable, depending, as it did, on some of the best known stereotypes in the culture. It was often large and brash and caused a flurry because of its apparent vulgarity. It seemed flatly to contradict the reigning art establishment (of Abstract Expressionism); appearing to be the reversion to representational art which is always predicted when abstraction dominates. It was easy to write about. Above all it had the perfect name, both modish and implying accessibility; it lent itself to catchy headlines and exhibition titles: 'Pop as Mod', 'Who is this Pop?', 'Pop goes the Easel', 'Snap, Crackle, Pop', 'Pop-Gun Weddings', etc.

In the event, the rapidity and wide scale of the success of Pop, which led commercial artists to reborrow ideas from it, monopolized the attention of most writers and made it impossible for others to treat it as seriously as an art as I believe it deserves. Of the main artists, I have only room to treat four, but the books in the reading list mention several others of equal, or almost equal quality. The four are chosen, paradoxically it

may seem, for their formal and conceptual interest. I am arguing, however, that Pop
Art takes its place in the stream of modernism, between Abstract Expressionism and
Minimal and Conceptual art and is not to be dismissed as an aberration or reversion.

JAMES ROSENQUIST (born 1933)

I begin with the youngest of the four, Rosenquist, who had made a living painting
billboards on a giant scale. The quotation from a statement (Appendix, pp. 15–16 is
for him unusually direct and apparently lacking in irony or evasion. It represents the
classical position of Pop:

1 'I would be a stronger painter if I made my decisions before I approached the
   canvas.'
2 A realization of the vitality of commercial advertising and visual communications
   and the effect of their scale and ubiquity.
3 A remaining commitment to fine art.

It is evident from his painting that he notices that the visual communications which
surround us in the city vary abruptly in their scale, focus, the apparent distance of the
object (far or extreme close-up), and whether they are in black and white or colour.
His pictures, like those of Phillips, combine images so as to produce a net of associations (Fig. 29). The associations here seem obvious—the well-known trio of food, sex
and cars—but there may be more subtle ones. The food is in the form of spaghetti
which hints both at the viscera beneath the skin and at visceral, Abstract Expressionist
painting. This part is in colour. If this really is a reference to art, could the central
band refer to naturalistic painting (or even Pop) and the upper one to formal abstraction? Is it an accident that the three images are animal, vegetable and mineral? I think
that in all probability, neither of these interpretations was in the mind of the artist
when he painted the picture, but I feel sure that the three images intentionally

Figure 29 James Rosenquist, *I love you with my Ford*, 1961, oil on board, two panels, 84¼ × 95½ ins (Moderna
Museet, Stockholm).

represent three different degrees of close-up: the most distant the car, the middle, sex, and the nearest food. This certainly appears to be an allegory.

However, even if the meanings are not as simple as this, Rosenquist's formal devices suggest an additive type of reading. The pictures are apparently assembled like a collage but the images do not overlap. (In other pictures they do overlap to some degree but remain orthogonal and there is no suggestion of elements combining into a formal unit.) Each element tends to occupy a regular, picture-shaped rectangle cutting across the real vertical divisions of the canvas, but changes of style between one and another are not dramatic, they are not the subject of the painting. It is clear therefore that each section has its own content. Although the painting resembles a collage it is entirely painted. This allows the changes of scale, which are fundamental, but it also asserts that we are looking at a veritable picture which is essential to the metaphor which he refers to in his last sentence.

CLAES OLDENBURG (born 1929)

Read the text by Oldenburg in Chipp, pp. 585–87 and also the manifesto written before Pop was defined as a movement in the Appendix, p. 16. The latter is a passionate appeal for the fusion of art and life, but the former is more generally relevant to Pop. It even attempts a definition, a very good one: 'We are all talking about making impersonality a style, which is what I think characterises Pop Art. . . .' Note that impersonal here does not mean dispassionate, it means (see the line at the top of the page) '. . . bringing in an image you did not create'. Oldenburg's images are not from the museum but from the supermarket. He exhibited and sold his work in simulated stores with a miscellany of goods. However these images are for Oldenburg simply shapes which may have a multitude of meanings. His position is almost the converse of that of Hamilton. The object is remade by the artist, usually on a different scale, so that it is stripped of its merely conventional uses and meanings and becomes a universal vehicle, a complex metaphor (see the third and last excerpts in Chipp).

Exercise

Study Figure 30 and note down the references you find in it. (These need not be what you think the artist intended.)

Discussion

The things I think of are: a pouffe as big as a double bed; a pair of lips with tongue between; the upper part, a beret or an ice pack; seen from the top, a target.

Exercise

Consider and note down its physical or formal properties.

Discussion

The most striking thing about it is, of course, its size. It shares with much minimal sculpture (see pp. 63–66) the fact that it is large enough to obstruct physically any room it is in. This is a conscious factor for Oldenburg: 'My work makes a great demand on a collector. I have tried to make it in every way so that anyone who comes into contact with it is greatly inconvenienced. That is to say, made aware of its existence, and of my principles.' The sculpture is conspicuously soft like a feather bed. The result of this is that the form is variable within the fixed limits of the skin. I have referred to the way that in conventional sculpture (see Henry Moore, p. 27) the surface generates the volume. Here the surface is an independent element, a skin of fixed area and shape, like a coat of paint, but of variable curvature and silhouette. The internal mass of stuffing acts on the skin to help determine the actual shape and both are visibly affected by gravity. The softness of the form implies the possibility of transformation. The sculpture can become something else. This agrees with Oldenburg's idea of bringing out the analogies between objects.

Figure 30 Claes Oldenburg, *Giant Hamburger*, 1962, painted sailcloth stuffed with foam, approximately 52 × 84 ins diameter (Art Gallery of Ontario).

ROY LICHTENSTEIN (born 1923)

In his paintings of the early 1960s Lichtenstein represents Pop Art at its most blatant. He is also one of those artists who can speak with absolute clarity and precision about his art. I shall leave him, therefore, largely to speak for himself (see the Appendix, pp. 16–17 and Plate 16 and Fig. 31). Figure 31 is one of those paintings which are not based on commercial sources but make a more or less direct comment on high art. In this case the comment is on the Abstract Expressionist cult of the brush stroke described by Greenberg as the 'Tenth Street touch': 'The stroke left by a loaded brush or knife frays out, when the stroke is long enough, into streaks, ripples and specks of paint.' Such a brush stroke, at once an emblem of involvement with the material and of unfettered, spontaneous self-expression, is treated by Lichtenstein as an *object*, almost a still life, to be painted. He reinforces the irony by doing it in the style of the comics but brings it back into the field of fine art by using paint and working on the large scale of the Abstract Expressionists themselves.

Exercise

On the basis of the quoted texts and of the pictures reproduced, relate Lichtenstein's art to some of the principal concerns and devices of the Abstract Expressionists:

1 the expression of the most profound or unconscious feelings through the spontaneous act of painting;

2 the all-over marking of the canvas and the avoidance of the illusion of figures in space;

3 the avoidance of preconceived style.

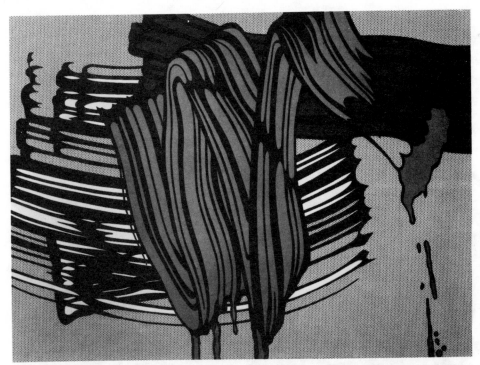

Figure 31 Roy Lichtenstein, *Big Painting No. 6*, 1965, oil, 92 × 129 ins (Kunstsammlung Nordrhein-West-falen, Düsseldorf).

Discussion

1   Lichtenstein 'pretends' to avoid expressing his own feelings and chooses a style which appears to be borrowed from commercial hacks. Nothing could seem less spontaneous. However, he often selects subjects of poignant, if hackneyed, emotion. There is no reason to believe that these emotions are in themselves any less profound, any less human, than those expressed by, say, Pollock. They are expressed in paint, but through a complex set of references: the original subject (a drowning girl) the original style (a comic) and variations on that style. The purport of this seems to be that expression demands conventions and that even Abstract Expressionists created and used style, willy-nilly.

2   In so far as a Lichtenstein painting purports to be a copy of a two-dimensional object, such as a frame from a comic book, it is axiomatically 'all-over', for this object is the whole picture and has no space round it. The surface is flat so there is no fore-ground and no background; the effect is emphasized by the 'benday' dots which often cover the canvas evenly. However we read the picture as a representation of objects. This is true in spite of the crude convention which gives the momentary forms of the water a brittle and flat permanence equal to that of the head. Such a convention, with its minimal three-dimensional effect, itself comes closer than most forms of high art to the respect for the two-dimensional surface, while, by virtue of its very convention-ality, maximizing the references to what is outside—that is, 'life'. If this seems obscure, consider written words, which are entirely conventional but which, because of that fact, have no other function than to describe the world.

3   In these pictures there is an obvious style and a hidden one. The obvious style is, of course, that of the comic book or advertisement (real or imagined) on which it is based; however, such a style, just because it is quoted, cannot be condemned as an ingrained habit of the painter, nor as the unique handiwork of an artist, to be sold at a high price because of its uniqueness. As in the painting of Hamilton, this style plays something like the role of the subject in earlier painting but there is only one style represented. Lichtenstein paints a picture of this style in his own style, varying the thickness and curvature of lines and the profile of shaped areas as he works. This process is, paradoxically, not unlike the continuous response to what is happening on the canvas that is characteristic of Abstract Expressionist methods. Needless to

say any such resemblance should not be exaggerated. Pop art does offend existing modernist canons by reintroducing images, by resorting to debased prototypes and by a sort of methodicalness and impersonality. At the same time it appears to recognize or pay homage to the principal 'rules' of Abstract Expressionism by turning them upside down. It often seems to demonstrate that a rule can be simultaneously obeyed and flouted, as in the case of the 'all-over' quality of both types of painting.

ANDY WARHOL (born *c.* 1928)

If Lichtenstein represents the very centre of Pop art, Warhol represents the extreme. He has made films, directed a pop group, written books and made sculptures but his most consistent art work is his life style. Although he constantly asserts that he is just like everyone else or that anyone could do his art, there is no mistaking the fact that he is a superstar (to use the term that he coined). Although he appears to repudiate invention, he is, I believe, unquestionably one of the very small number of truly original artists of his time. Read the texts in the Appendix but bear in mind that the

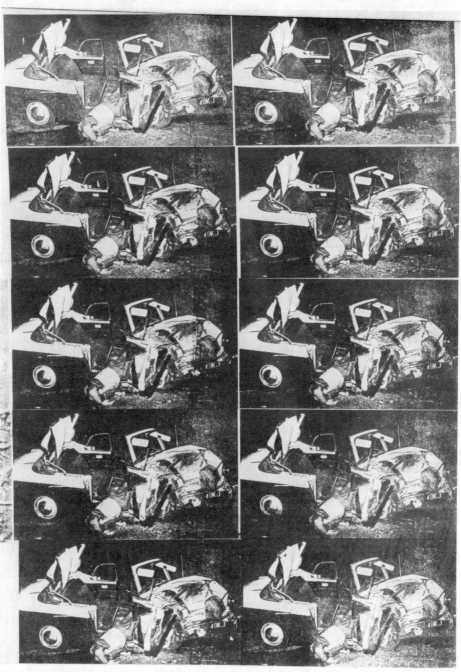

Figure 32 Andy Warhol, *Green Disaster*, 1963, oil, $81\frac{1}{4} \times 90\frac{1}{2}$ ins (Carl Ströher Collection, Hessisches Landes-museum, Darmstadt).

57

Figure 33 Andy Warhol, *100 Campbell Soup Cans*, 1963, oil, 72 × 52 ins (Carl Ströher Collection, Hessisches Landesmuseum, Darmstadt).

interview, pp. 17–18, must have been drastically edited. Anyone who has heard Warhol talk knows that he could not possibly have spoken as fluently and as purposefully as this. Unlike Lichtenstein, for example, his temperament does not allow him to produce anything like a linear argument. I make this point not to impugn the quotation, which certainly gives an accurate account of his position at the time, but to point out that his way of speaking is entirely of a piece with his painting. Plate 17 and Figures 32 and 33 represent quite well almost the full range of his painting. One omission is a wallpaper, repeating the head of a cow taken from an advertisement, covering the walls of the exhibiting gallery. 1962–64 (when he turned to film making) were his most inventive years as a painter. In 1962 be began to paint by means of screen printing; in this process an image can be photographed directly onto a woven screen (originally of silk) through which paint or printing ink can be pressed by means of a squeegee like that used to wipe windows. The image is thus transferred to canvas or paper. This technique had been developed for commercial purposes and then used as a way of making prints by artists such as Hamilton and Paolozzi, but I believe that

Warhol was the first to use it for producing paintings, The significance of this is that the image appears in essentially the same form as it appears outside art and without any obvious intervention by the artist, except that he has chosen it, generally enlarged it and brought it into the fine-art frame of reference. Further, Warhol almost always uses images that have been in effect already chosen by the public, that is, the most popular: Marilyn Monroe, Campbell's soup, dramatic accidents, dollar bills, etc. This is a still more extreme form of the type of non-choice described above by Oldenburg and is the opposite of the type of non-choice adopted by the Abstract Expressionists: the public is symbolically substituted for the individual or collective subconscious. The substitution, however, makes it clear that the two are not altogether mutually exclusive; there is clearly a degree of subconscious motivation in, for example, Warhol's *Green Disaster* (Fig. 32).

Another type of apparent 'non-choice' governs the type of composition, or rather, 'non-composition' used by Warhol. Plate 16 shows a centrally placed image related to those of Noland (Plate 9) while Figures 32 and 33 repeat images in simple rank and file which may be compared with the arrangement of elements in Figures 38–41 which are discussed later. Although rectilinear, this is the opposite to the kind of carefully judged and asymmetrical composition of a Mondrian. The composition, that is the spatial relationship between elements, is reduced almost to nothing by a process of banalization. It cannot be altogether eliminated (while there is more than one colour on the canvas) but it can be made as uninteresting as possible by adopting the most commonplace configuration, one that, like the subject matter, the artist cannot be thought to have invented. In the case of a painting such as the *Disaster* which is taken from images which, unlike soup tins, are not normally seen in serried ranks, the effect of the banality of the composition is to heighten the horror of the subject. It seems to imply a mindless repetition of the event and so to deny any singularity to the victims of the disaster. Warhol often denies that there is any comment in his art but in this instance the comment is certainly there, even if it is no more than the result of the direct simulation of a commonplace in the sort of society that sells millions of news-papers on the basis of such images repeated with the insistence of a penance (Warhol came from a strongly Catholic family). Another point that must be made about War-hol's screen paintings is that (like the later paintings of Rauschenberg or the photo-montages of the Russian Constructivists) they use photographs as a substitute for reality rather than as a mere representation of it. This, too, is a simple reflection of a commonplace, for it is evident that for most of us the world consists of a series of events taking place in the newspapers and on television (as MacLuhan and others have described). We have an almost complete faith in the objectivity of photographs; Warhol draws attention to this by, among other things, the irregular way he passes the paint through the screen. The photograph is given by this means, which exaggerates the degradation normal to newspaper pictures, an accidental or damaged look. In other words, the photograph itself is treated as an object. This suggestion is analogous to the effect of the brush stroke in Expressionist painting or to the deliberate incom-pleteness of some of Peter Blake's paintings (see pp. 49–50).

Exercise

Discuss the concept of high art and low art and the position taken by Hamilton, Lichtenstein and Warhol in relation to the two.

Discussion

I have used the term 'high' art more or less interchangeably with 'fine art' (painting). From the context you may also deduce that it implies high-brow or avant-garde art or even, specifically, modernism. 'Low' art includes commercial art but also, in some contexts, the secondary, derivative or even academic kinds of fine art. There is an implication that 'high art' is better than 'low art' but the coining of a symmetrical pair of terms implies an irony or doubt that the previous distinctions such as 'good art' and 'bad art', 'fine art' and 'commercial art' or 'original art' and 'Kitsch' did not.

Pop artists generally have chosen to use images derived more or less directly from 'low-art' sources, but over a wide spectrum. In the case of Hamilton, these images come often from the upper ranges of design and graphics produced by highly trained designers, creators of style, who are speaking to a sophisticated public. He does not often use such material unaltered and combines it with high art techniques and references, to Pollock, Mondrian and Cézanne. It implies a continuum of talent and significance between the two but is unequivocally 'high art' itself.

Lichtenstein in the early 1960s chose images and styles from the lowest of the low: comics and pulp magazines. The fine-art adjustments other than the scale and use of canvas and paint are not obvious and have been overlooked by many people. Lichtenstein is answering the challenge to make art out of the unlikeliest sources and the same is paradoxically the case when he makes a painting out of a reproduction of a well-known modern masterpiece by, for example, Picasso. What could be further from art, in the eyes of the cognoscenti, than a reproduction of a great painting? However, when regarded closely, a painting by Lichtenstein turns out to be art in just the same way—in the characteristics of handling and form-making—that any high-art painting is.

Warhol's material is often even more debased. It is newspaper photographs, publicity stills and packaging which nobody regards as art at all but which, nevertheless, attract as much attention and occupy as significant a role in the culture as any work of art. They are the imagery chosen by the public, but when Warhol chose them they at once became features of the interior decoration of the houses of the art-loving public. They began to fill their living rooms first with real Brillo boxes and the giant tins that food manufacturers sometimes use to advertise tinned foods, but soon shops began to sell specially made, imitation tins of the same type at fairly high prices. This dramatically exemplified the irony of Warhol's work and the dynamic of taste in the new vast middle-brow audience was demonstrated with uncanny clarity.

Minimalism

The artists Stella, Andre, Judd, LeWitt and to some degree Morris, produced closely related work in the early 1960s and it is this group that I shall describe under the heading of Minimalism. Of the five, four are sculptors and one, Stella, is a painter. Stella has developed under the influence of the Greenbergian tradition (see pp. 33–35 above) as a neo-Cubist but the sculptors are among the founders and heroes of Conceptual Art (see p. 72). All of them emerged from a period (however brief) as painters and so join the ranks of the painters turned sculptors who have dominated the medium in this century. None of them seems to create out of a sense of a struggle with a demanding material, as earlier sculptors have, including Smith and Caro (see above pp. 28–33).

Read Bruce Glaser's interview with Stella and Judd, in the Appendix, pp. 18–19. The most striking thing about it is that it expresses, even more strongly, an American chauvinism that goes back to Pollock and his contemporaries. Once more the Europeans are accused of composing pictures—of relational art.

Such a view is naive in the extreme, showing no awareness of the immense range of composition and decomposition explored by European artists. Think, for example, of Degas' 'camera angles', of Arp's random squares and Klee's grid-like drawings.

There is a curious passage in which Stella speaks of using the same designs as the Europeans but asserts that theirs are relational while his are not. In fighting his way out of this corner he speaks of symmetry as non-relational. Later he repudiates Pollock and de Kooning for similar reasons: making inflections with the paint. He aims at an absolutely unitary activity and a unitary experience on the part of the viewer. In this sense he is closer to Newman or Rothko than to Pollock.

FRANK STELLA (born 1936)

Looking at Stella's pictures (Figs 34 and 35) you will see that they are, of course, not absolutely unitary, but that the parts do not have an independent existence: they are elementary sub-divisions of the surface. In fact the width of the divisions is the width of the stretcher bars that support the canvas and this has led some writers to assert that the shape of the canvas (misleadingly called the 'literal' shape) governs the painted configuration (depicted shape). However this cannot be literally true, since it is unlikely that by working inwards from the edge, Stella could arrive at a neat finish at the centre. On the contrary, it is evident that the painted configuration, or its rhythm, determines the canvas shape, or that the two are worked out together before painting begins. In any event, there is such a complete integration that there can be no significant relational balancing of one internal shape against another.

At this date (1960) his pictures were always monochrome, the lines being left bare so that colour relationships were also reduced to a minimum.

Figure 34 shows part of an exhibition in which all the pictures were based on the same principles and made of the same paint, aluminium. Several of Stella's shows of about the same period have comprised sets of variations of this type. Cumulatively the pictures call attention to the generating principle or system on which they are based and this takes the place of the subject matter of earlier series such as Poussin's *Seven Sacraments*. In this respect it is interesting that Stella says (Appendix, p. 19) 'all I want anyone to get out of my paintings . . . is the fact that you can see the whole *idea* without any confusion . . . what you see is what you see.' Note that you see the *idea* and that the idea is what makes the whole painting. The idea and the image are as closely integrated as the image and the canvas. This is an assertion of the importance and self-sufficiency of the act of painting.

Figure 34 Frank Stella, installation of the exhibition at the Leo Castelli Gallery, New York, 1960, showing left to right: *Kingsbury Run*, 1960, aluminium paint on canvas, 78 × 78 ins; *Newstead Abbey*, 1960, aluminium paint on canvas, 120 × 72 ins; *Avicenna*, 1960, aluminium paint on canvas, 72 × 72 ins (Leo Castelli Gallery, New York; photo: Rudolph Burckhardt).

Figure 35 Frank Stella, *Jasper's Dilemma*, 1962/63, alkyd on canvas, 77 × 130 ins (Private collection).

However, the 'idea' may be quite complicated without 'confusion'. In *Jasper's Dilemma* (Fig. 35) the title refers to Jasper Johns' oscillation between coloured and grisaille paintings but the system seems to be a comment on Stella's own. The painting is in two halves of which the geometry of one exactly mirrors the other. In each case Stella begins at a corner which is the one at the bottom centre of the combined canvases. He draws a band upwards, makes a mitre at the first corner, goes round to the next where he makes another mitre and so on. It is the fact that the first stripe cannot begin with a mitre that produces the break in one of the diagonals and the two small triangles in the centre. This apparent 'mistake' is evidence of the sequential nature of the process starting with the real edge of the canvas. The square on the left is coloured in a repeated sequence of eleven hues based on their order in the spectrum —a borrowed system, like those of Pop Art. The right-hand square has a similar repeated system of seven shades of grey. Seven is the traditional number of colours seen in a spectrum but the effect of the choice of seven and eleven is that the same colour or shade appears successively in the next quarter clockwise to the one it has previously appeared in. All this can easily be worked out, but, in the end, nothing is determined except that that is the system used. The picture therefore remains perfectly self-contained. All that remains outside is the significance of adopting such a system.

The minimalist search for purity seems to be a self-consciously 'American' attitude deriving in the most obvious way from their traditional distrust of sophistication. American artists value the single all-out statement—equivalent, as I have suggested, to the shoot-out in old cowboy movies—and they have made the cowboy's or farmhand's jeans into the artist's universal uniform (more recently of course these have spread throughout youth culture).

DONALD JUDD (born 1928)

In the discussion referred to above (Appendix, p. 18) Judd is also pushed into a sort of contradiction. He condemns the 'Europeans' for preconceiving their work and then has to admit that his own is preconceived. In fact, anyone looking at a sculpture by Judd will see that it is preconceived to a much greater degree than any earlier European work (Figs 36–37). Judd gets himself out of the impasse by equating reasoning (preconceiving) with the relating of parts. He characterizes his own reasoning as

Figure 36 Donald Judd, sculpture 'untitled', 1967, as installed in the garden of the Albright Knox Museum, Buffalo, 1967; eight stainless-steel cubes 48 × 48 × 48 ins (Photo: Michael Compton, with permission of Leo Castelli Gallery, New York).

63

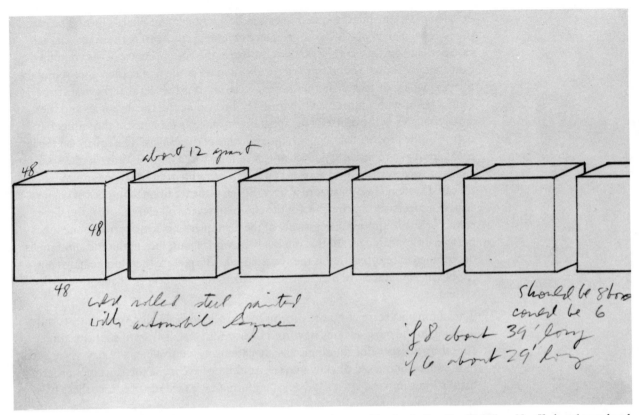

Figure 37 Donald Judd, drawing for 'untitled', 1967 (Los Angeles County Museum of Art, lent by Leo Castelli Gallery, New York, and reproduced with their permission).

'much smaller,' by which he means purely tactical: the thought necessary to construct the piece. In another passage he refers to a box: '. . . it does have an order, but it's not so ordered that it's the dominant quality. The more parts a thing has, the more important order becomes, and finally order becomes more important than anything else'. What Judd is after is to have 'one quality. The main things are alone and are more intense, clear and powerful'. This position is very close to that of Stella and can be seen again as a logical outcome of Pollock's all-over pictures of the late 1940s.

A box-like sculpture of this kind need not be made by the sculptor himself. It can be made by a workman and this includes the sculptor in another role. It consists of a specification for material, dimensions, number of parts and the relationship between them (Fig. 37). Such a specification is perfectly unambiguous both to the maker and to the person looking at the result. In certain of these works the number of units may be varied according to the situation in which they are placed. The work of art is therefore not a final concept but the manifestation of a set of rules capable of generating a series. Judd is concerned with the real space in which his works stand; they are large enough or so displayed that they can articulate the space they occupy, as a large piece of furniture does. In the example illustrated, you can see another characteristic way in which the relationship is asserted and made use of. The shiny, stainless steel sides of the boxes reflect the light and colour of their surroundings; the sides are tinged with the grass, the top with sky.

CARL ANDRE (born 1932)

In Andre's work the sense of an intimate relationship to the space in which the sculpture is made or seen is even more important than in Judd's. He tends to move around, using materials which he finds to hand and assembling them in simple configurations (Fig. 38). This work is made of commercial precast concrete blocks. The whole floor is covered, except for a set of rectangles made by taking out in each case 30 bricks; the dimensions of the rectangles must necessarily be the dimensions of the blocks multiplied by the factors of 30. Taking the length and breadth in that order, you have the complete set, beginning on the right with 30 × 1, along the left wall 15 × 2, in the middle 10 × 3, and so on until you get to 1 × 30 along the back wall. This was a piece specially made for a specific gallery. Its converse, which can be sold, is a set of, say, 120 similar bricks or slabs which the owner arranges according to appropriate factors for his room. In a public gallery, with more space, it may be stipulated that they are arranged in each proportion in turn, at regular intervals of weeks or days.

It is significant that this introduces the notion of the owner's responsibility according to his means. You will recall that Oldenburg claimed to make demands on his collectors but here there is a more specific demand; Andre has more recently sold works for a proportion of the owner's annual income. As a result of the protests over the Vietnam war and the world-wide student 'revolutions' of 1968–69 he became politicized. He has taken a position against the trading in works of art as commodities, although not a consistent one; his sculptures are bought and sold. However, he often makes them virtually unsaleable as *Cut* is. He uses materials like bricks or scrap metal which symbolize a non-precious art (Fig. 39) and his variable pieces, constructed out of patterns which he has not invented. (He has made sculpture in the fields using bales of hay which returned to their agricultural use afterwards.)

Exercise

Many people feel that a sculpture of the kind described above is 'just a load of bricks'. On the other hand it has been defended as being meaningful in its context. Note down points relevant to this contradiction.

Figure 38 Carl Andre, *Cuts*, 1967, assembled in the Dwan Gallery, Los Angeles, concrete sculpture, 2 × 360 × 504 ins (Photo: courtesy of John Weber Gallery, New York).

Figure 39 Carl Andre, *Stile*, proposed 1960 executed 1975, four pieces of cedar 12 × 12 × 36 ins (Photo: John Ferrari, courtesy of John Weber Gallery, New York).

Discussion

1   The sculpture is indeed just a load of bricks arranged in a simple but specific fashion. Andre might say with Stella: 'You can see the whole idea without any confusion. . . . What you see is what you see.' What the critics say is literally true and corresponds to part of the artist's intentions.

2   By reducing the materials to ready-made units and by letting the form of these determine the overall shape which consists of simple multiples of them, Andre limits the idea as well as the physical characteristics to what can be seen, and is immediately recognizable. The idea cannot be detached from the objects.

3   Such a work is a product of a long tradition of asserting that a work of art is basically a physical object in its own right, independent of any references to what is outside it, although works of art have been constantly found to contain such references.

4   Andre goes close to producing an art which is non-referential but in the end he fails to produce 'just a heap of bricks' arranged according to a schoolchild's repertoire of factors. At the least he makes reference to the tradition cited above and to the tradition of non-relational art cited in respect of Newman and others. He also makes reference to Duchamp's tradition of presenting as art the product of a non-aesthetic process and to political considerations of art as work and art as commodity.

SOL LEWITT (born 1928)

In the work of LeWitt the relationship between the idea which generates a work of art and the resultant work is central. He may be regarded as the classical case of one type of Conceptual artist while retaining some of the same characteristics of the Minimal artists I have been discussing. The quotation from LeWitt's 'Serial Project No. 1' (Appendix, p. 21) is a general statement describing the kinds of systems used by Stella, Judd and Andre. See also the quotations from his 'Paragraphs on Conceptual Art' and 'Sentences on Conceptual Art' (Appendix, pp. 19–20). LeWitt describes the *idea* as the 'machine that makes the art' but asserts that the art is purposeless. This seems to mean that the artist adopts a rigorous method which will generate the work but that he has no end (purpose) in mind. The idea is adopted intuitively or irrationally and the end result is to be responded to just as the viewer wishes: the element of expression is eliminated from the work. LeWitt believes that to make adjustments during the execution of the piece is to open the way to the 'capricious and subjective' and leads to compromise and to repetition of past results. He equates formal with rational art, which he asserts repeats itself, and he clearly aligns himself with the irrational: 'Illogical judgements lead to new experience' and 'Irrational thoughts should be followed absolutely and logically'. All of this reads like a demonstration that the beliefs of the Abstract Expressionists or even the Surrealists can be turned inside-out and still have validity. He shares with them an aversion to the relational adjustment of forms and to reason, but argues that these can only be avoided by control and predetermination.

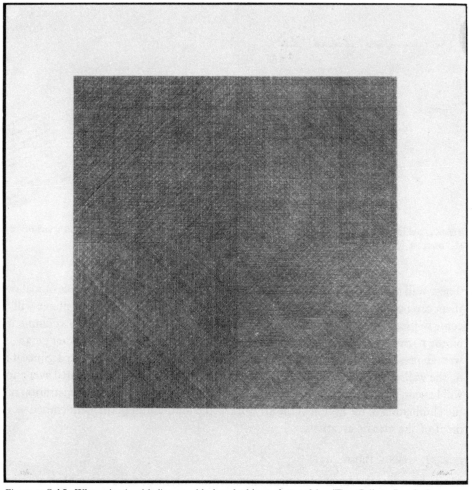

Figure 40 Sol LeWitt, print (untitled), 1971, black and white, 20⅛ × 20⅛ ins (Tate Gallery, London).

I illustrate two works (Figs 40 and 41); both are flat, although LeWitt is regarded as a sculptor and makes three-dimensional objects. I have chosen these because they are best suited to reproduction here. In Figure 41 LeWitt sets out in tabular form all the possible combinations of vertical, horizontal, dexter and sinister, diagonal lines. Figure 40 raises a rather different issue. This is a book, the pages of which are marked with lines according to a set of prescriptions, which are both used to control the drawing of it and remain written on the page. The viewer both reads the prescription and looks at the drawing. It becomes evident that the prescription or title is adequate to determine the drawing process but does not exhaust the characteristics of the physical object that results. Drawings of the same type are executed directly on walls; the shape, lighting and texture of the wall, the composition of the pencil lead, the pressure and speed of drawing, the hand that executes it (which need not be that of the artist), etc., all play a part. In considering the relation of the prescription to the drawing, one learns something about the meaning or usage of words like 'from', 'to' and 'towards' and about concepts like 'corner' or 'mid-point'.

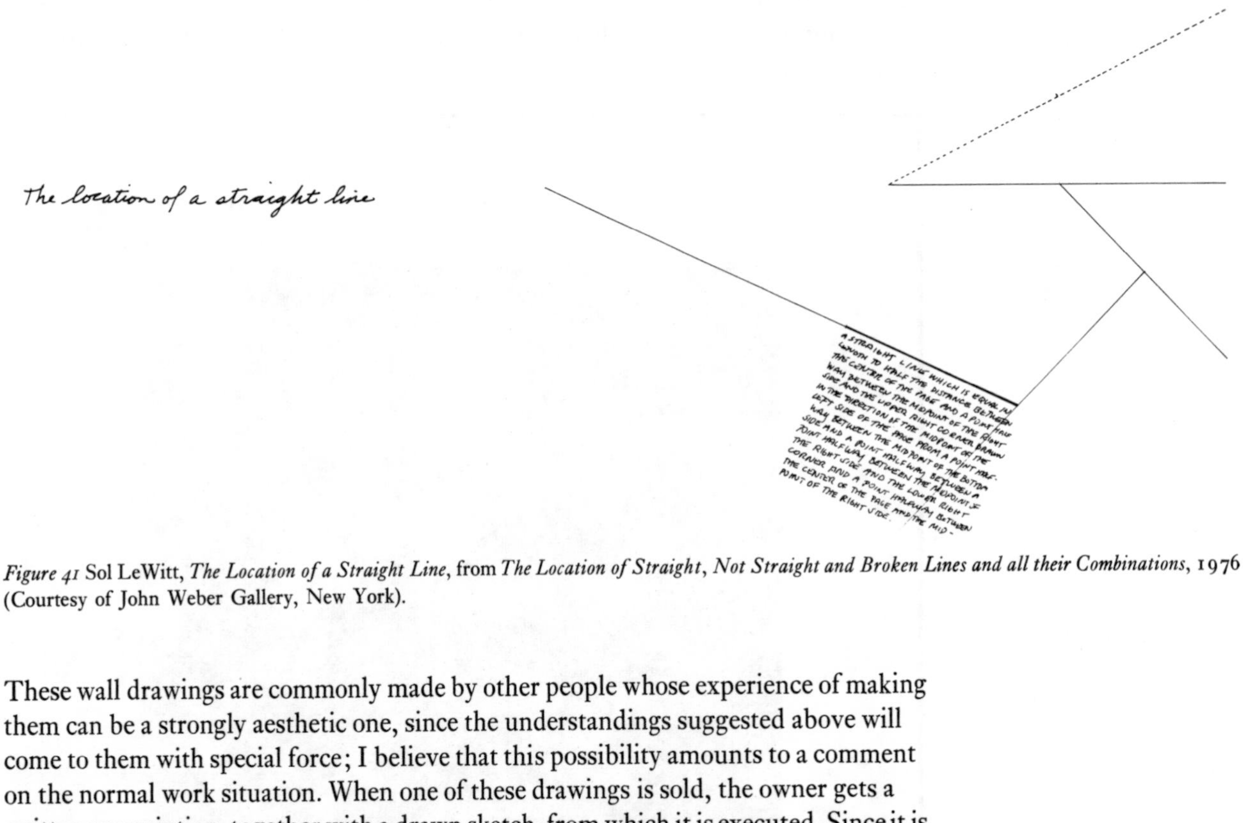

The location of a straight line

Figure 41 Sol LeWitt, *The Location of a Straight Line*, from *The Location of Straight, Not Straight and Broken Lines and all their Combinations*, 1976 (Courtesy of John Weber Gallery, New York).

These wall drawings are commonly made by other people whose experience of making them can be a strongly aesthetic one, since the understandings suggested above will come to them with special force; I believe that this possibility amounts to a comment on the normal work situation. When one of these drawings is sold, the owner gets a written prescription, together with a drawn sketch, from which it is executed. Since it is on the wall, if any other use has to be made of the wall, the drawing is painted over and will have to be redrawn for another showing. This may be read as a demonstration of the elimination of the notion of the art work as the unique and permanent embodiment of the artist's creativity.

ROBERT MORRIS (born 1931)

Morris is unlike the American artists discussed already, who tend to establish a characteristic, usually a simple and easily recognizable image or method, and to work at it for several years, if not a lifetime; a reflection of what amounts to an American national passion for integrity above all other virtues. Morris has frequently worked in several quite different manners at the same time, different not only in the morphology of the works produced but in the kinds of ideas which underlie them. There remains, naturally, a consistency at a deeper level. Morris is also a representative of the weakening in the xenophobia of American art; from the late 1960s there is a renewed fusion of American and European traditions and a mutual respect among younger artists which has gone much further in the next generation of artists.

The reasons for this may lie in the exhaustion of the impetus which carried American art from Abstract Expressionism to the Minimalism of Stella but I think it also lies in the political and economic events of the period. The Vietnam war eroded and eventually destroyed (if only for a short period) American self-righteousness, easily discernible in the country's artists as well as its journalists and politicians. The inability of the American political system to sustain either growth or a fair degree of economic equality, turned large numbers of the young and the intellectually active away from American capitalism and towards various kinds of European socialism and anarchism. The events of 1968 caused many to think European. At the same time it was becoming obvious that West Germany, France, Japan and other countries were rapidly catching up economically; West Germany became an art market of almost equal importance to the east coast of the USA.

European galleries and museums, especially those in Holland and West Germany, with their lack of metropolitan prejudices, have often found it easier to adapt to the great and rapid changes in the forms of art which will be described in the next section and especially to work with artists on the basis of offering them a space in which to do their work rather than merely to hang ready-made works of art. Of all this, Morris (although not by any means alone in his generation) has been a barometer.

Read first of all the quotation on pp. 22–23 of the Appendix, which is among the most sophisticated artists' statements of the Minimalist position. This statement corresponds to the work shown at the Green Gallery in New York in 1964 (Fig. 42).

Figure 42 Robert Morris, exhibition at the Green Gallery, New York, 1964 (Leo Castelli Gallery, New York; photo: Rudolph Burckhardt).

Figure 43 Robert Morris, *Felts* Exhibition, Leo Castelli Gallery, New York, 1968 (Leo Castelli Gallery, New York).

The term *gestalt* derives from the psychology of perception. It means that which the brain tends to see as a whole, even completing what is deficient. 98 degrees of arc of a circle are seen as a circle. Morris uses the term in the sense of a geometrical *gestalt* of this type but there are biological ones such as the human face. In addition to what he says, note that the *gestalt*s are as nearly as possible projections of mental objects. They do not pretend to be solids, to have mass, or to be permanent. On the other hand, they occupy a lot of space. The slab floating on the right, called *Cloud*, obstructs the space beneath for any person more than about five feet tall, and the pyramid in the corner both prevents access to that corner and forms an uneasy link between the two walls and the floor. It has another property to which the statement draws our attention, namely that only one side is visible and this must always be well illuminated if the gallery is lit. Degrees of light, therefore, do not distinguish its sides. The remaining three sides are implied only by the planes of the walls and the floor, to which they run parallel at a short distance. Briefly, we reconstruct a solid from the bare minimum of visual information. Works of this type, together with those of Judd, were described by the critic Barbara Rose as 'thoroughly conceptual' on the grounds that they could be executed by others and were 'willed into being'.

Another sculpture (not illustrated) by Morris, includes a card index filled with cards which refer to every mental and physical act in the making of the piece, for example: card 1 'Accident 7/12/62 1:30–2:03 pm. Three minutes late from lunch due to trip (See Trip 1)'; turning to the card representing Trip 1 you find: '7/12/62 1:30–2:03 pm. To Daniels Stationery to look at file boxes', etc. The interest of this piece is that it identifies the work of art with a mental and physical process in a more explicit way than before and that it incorporates that process by means of documents. Another sculpture had been a box containing a tape recorder which played the sounds of sawing, nailing etc. that were made as the box was being constructed. Both works are also reflexive, that is they refer to themselves, a characteristic that becomes common in Conceptual art but which can be traced back to Duchamp's *Bride stripped Bare by her Bachelors, even* (see Unit 13). Other sculptures of this type by Morris include an electric bulb coupled to a meter so that the meter registers the amount of electricity consumed by the bulb during the exhibition and a wall panel with four counters on which are set the distances of the piece from the floor, ceiling, and two adjacent walls. Yet another work is self-referential in a different way and is the reversal of a Duchamp idea. It comprises a sculpture that Morris had exhibited before, together with a certificate withdrawing its status as a work of art.

While continuing to make objects of both the minimal and this didactic kind, Morris began to work out the implications of some earlier pieces made of rope. These might be of felt, cut into 'minimal' geometric shapes but allowed to fall into heaps at random, according to the chance intervention of, say, gallery owners (Fig. 43) and gravity on the physical properties of the material, or they may be heaps of inchoate materials collected according to some principle, such as the range of solid fuels available locally.

Some of Morris's works have an ecological reference. This may be the use of stock materials which can be used for other purposes after the exhibition or the placing of a humidifier in a desert to create a local climate with specific flora and fauna. More recently, Morris has designed 'observatories' comprising terraces and trenches, along which a person may walk or exercise and which are orientated to the sun and other celestial bodies in the way that Stonehenge is. All this can be seen as a gradual progression away from the art object towards a notion of art as a primitive cosmic experience.

Conceptual Art

In spite of the fact that most of the artists whose work I have described are still work-ing and that the traditions they represent have continued to produce interesting, sometimes very fine, artists, the last eight years or so have been dominated by a new tradition commonly referred to as Conceptual Art.

I have pointed several times to the stylistic diversity of post-war movements, but the diversity of Conceptual Art is even more extreme for reasons which derive directly from the very characteristics which have given it its name and which continue to give it vitality. The artists I will discuss are a mere sample, chosen partly on the basis of my judgement of quality but also in order to represent succinctly the range of work.

At its most basic level, Conceptual Art shifts the focus of attention from the art object to the idea. Of course art has always been the product of ideas, whether individually or culturally generated, conscious or unconscious, verbal or non-verbal. Conversely, even the most rarified Conceptual Art, as I shall show, retains a physical element, if only the sound of a voice in the air, and in many instances it is more conspicuously physical than a painting. There is an irony in the fact that it had taken several genera-tions of artists to establish the physicality of a painting (from Serusier to Noland) and half a generation to turn it upside down (from Rauschenberg or Klein to Conceptual Art).

Even so those artists who are described as Conceptual, do direct attention to the idea even when their work is most obviously physical in its manifestation. As I have asserted for Johns and Rauschenberg the medium in which they work is not a specific physical medium, still less a traditional one such as painting, but is art as a whole. The strategy is to bring an ever wider range of experience within the field of the aesthetic consciousness.

Duchamp spoke of giving a new *thought* to existing objects and the same may be said of many Conceptual artists if the term 'objects' may be stretched to include processes, activities and even thoughts themselves. However, there is often a specifically politi-cal or social element in the new art. It is felt by some that those who are in power, control society by controlling its symbols, both the physical symbol and the meaning which is attached to it. The Marxist notion of demystification (which often consists in substituting the obscure for the simple) is a model for certain artists, who aim so high as to wish to wrest this control for themselves, or at least to reveal the process in such a way that it could become subject to radical change (see later: Art and Language, Victor Burgin, John Latham and Hans Haacke). However, even where there is no such explicit or extreme aim, artists whose medium is 'Art' need to exercise the same degree of care and control over their medium as those whose medium is paint on canvas.

The medium of 'Art' includes the whole or parts of the 'system' as Duchamp and much later Rauschenberg, Klein, etc., began to demonstrate. One can only begin an inven-tory of the parts of the system, but it might include: the roles assigned to the artists, art work, galleries, collectors, critics, museums, by themselves, by each other and by outsiders; the aims, ideas, concepts, procedures, patterns of behaviour of each of these; the written, spoken and acted expressions by which exchanges are made; resources of materials, processes and information; the buildings, filing and account-ing systems, the schools, libraries, the public services, the meetings between people in which such exchanges are made and, above all, the social and political matrix, itself an enormously expanded network of the same type. Almost as fast as artists become aware of them, they are used, as artists have always used what pertained to their art, but they have used them up. It is as if the function of art were to reveal a thing by playing with it, and, having revealed, to pass on. Indeed, one of the artists, Donald Burgy, has said: 'What it means to be avant garde is to constantly waste cultural forms; to throw them away; an obsolescence not of forms but of contexts as well.'

Exercise

Define for yourself the phrase 'avant garde' and comment on the statement by Donald Burgy just quoted.

Discussion

I believe the conventional notion of an avant garde includes:
1   The primacy of novelty—it constantly explores new forms or new perceptions or new areas of consideration.
2   The idea of the leader and the herd—what is revealed can be passed on to followers and eventually pervades the culture.
3   An assessment of quality based on these—what has been done cannot be done again and pretend to be as good.
4   An evolutionary view of art—at any given time culture is going in a certain direction and only what tends in that direction but is ahead of the march is truly creative.

In relation to painting, avant-gardism can apply to subject matter, content and form or style but above all to the last, especially in the mid twentieth century. By this time variations in form had largely supplanted subject matter and had become the medium through which content was expressed. Forms were wasted, but contexts were not, because context was not the focus of attention.

As an illustration, Duchamp can be said to have wasted a context, that of the salon-type exhibition, in his *Urinal*; to a degree he also wasted the signature, by signing it 'R. Mutt'. As a further example, it could be said that the concept of the unconscious as a context for art was wasted by the Surrealists and Abstract Expressionists, but the unconscious was a subject matter or a means, not the primary mode of the art.

However Conceptual Art uses context far more intimately: it is an art of gesture or utterance in context, which comments on, raises to consciousness and aims to change context; context has become the subject matter and the focus of attention. It is precisely this which is wasted as each artist seeks out new contexts to manipulate. Instead of wasting styles, artists use up the most general concerns of society such as ecology, trade unionism, racialism, sexual roles, etc.

It is true that these concerns have been wasted only in relation to art but avant-gardism seems to have wasted some of its own essential elements. It is possible to think not only of individual subject matters, contents and styles being wasted by avant-gardism, but also of subject matter, content and style themselves being exhausted. If media and context are to be exhausted equally quickly (and the likelihood is that they would be exhausted more quickly, being more general) avant-gardism would soon run out of material. In fact, of course, there are many fine and great artists whose work is avant-garde only in the sense of being personal or of inspiring imitators. Avant-gardism certainly has been a force in art but it is by no means the only one or the most important.

Conceptual art is also reflexive and synoptic; it feeds on itself and on other art. It has inherited forms, processes and sensibilities from other movements: one can cite the substitution of photograph for object from Pop Art or from Russian Constructivism, the use of numerical and geometric systems from Minimal or Kinetic art, the use of chance from Abstract Expressionism or Surrealism, performance from Futurism, Dada or Happenings, fetishism from Surrealism, the incorporation of found objects, again from Surrealism or from Assemblage, the problematic of the art object from Dada, even the substitution of written works and the life-style of the artist for objects from the cases of, say, Whistler, Wyndham Lewis, Marinetti or Duchamp. This does not imply that Conceptual Art is exceptionally eclectic or derivative, only that it is constantly exploring the field and definitions of art. Moreover, it suggests that there is little point in looking for the origins of the movement because they are almost everywhere. With the almost universal teaching of art history and also a smattering of sociology, history of film, politics, etc. by art schools, as well as a wide range of crafts like photography, sound recording and various forms of printing, taught not as trades to be practised for a lifetime but as resources, art schools have responded to and perhaps encouraged a very wide notion of the role of an artist. Recently a sociological study of teachers and students found the universal assumption that the business of the teachers was to further the personal development of the students 'in whatsoever direction this may lead.'

The evolution from Assemblage, Pop and Minimal Art to Conceptual, has depended upon and prompted an evolution in the methods of dealer's galleries and museums or public galleries. In the case of the latter, this can be traced back to the early nineteenth century when the first museums of modern art were formed, so that new art could be held until its quality was established by consensus and the best works would then join the old masters in the great museums like the Louvre or the National Gallery. This system proved unable to cope with art which defied the conventions in a radical way, beginning with the Impressionists, and so there grew up specialized museums to represent and promote avant-garde art of which the Museum of Modern Art in New York is the most complete. From this, it was but a step to enabling artists actually to make, as well as to exhibit, their work. I have given an instance in Tinguely's *Homage to New York*, 1960 (see p. 38); another might be the *Fire Wall* of Yves Klein in 1961. Such works are costly in money or organizational time and as ephemeral as carnivals. They negate the notion of a museum as a storehouse of works of imperishable quality.

Dealers likewise have collaborated in the creation of unsaleable works or events. I have cited Klein's show *Le Vide* at the Galérie Iris Clert in 1958 (see p. 40); this was a special case, but a number of galleries, of which Konrad Fischer in Düsseldorf has been the leading example, have, from 1967, systematically based their programme on the practice of inviting artists to come and make or devise an exhibit for the specific space and occasion. I have cited the Andre floor sculpture (Fig. 38) at the Dwan Gallery and mentioned the LeWitt wall drawings of which examples have been shown at the Lisson Gallery. Both are galleries which work regularly in this way.

Seth Siegelaub, in New York, has acted as a kind of gallery proprietor without a gallery. In 1968 he published a collection of works of art in the form of duplicated sheets, allowing each artist twenty-five pages to present his own 'piece'. (This word has gradually replaced the specific terms 'painting', 'sculpture' and even 'work of art' as their implications and limitations have been exceeded.) The following year he presented an exhibition which existed only as a catalogue including pieces by Weiner, Huebler and others discussed below.

In 1971, Siegelaub and others drew up an 'Artists' Reserved Rights Sale Agreement' designed to give artists a degree of control over their work after it has been sold and a percentage of the profit on resale. This last is justified by a clause in the preamble: 'Whereas the Collector and Artist recognize that the value of the Work, unlike that of an ordinary chattel, is and will be affected by each and every other work of art that the Artist has created and will hereafter create'.

Works of art in the form of publications are not new; consider, for example, William Blake's books and Blaise Cendrars' and Sonia Delaunay's *La Prose du Transsibérien* which have combined poetry with visual art. In the 1960s, however, cheaply produced books began to appear consisting of nothing but images. The most remarkable were perhaps those of Ed Ruscha of Los Angeles, influenced no doubt by the banality of Warhol's photographically-derived images. The best known of Ruscha's books are

Twenty-six Gasoline Stations, 1962 (photographs of 26 commonplace garages), and *Various Small Fires and Milk* (photographs of a cigarette lighter burning, a gas ring, a match, etc. and a glass of milk). One of the features of these books is the surprising literalness of the title; in this they compare with the title descriptions of LeWitt's drawings (Fig. 41). The Art and Project Gallery in Amsterdam has consistently published works of art in the form of a Bulletin which is mailed all over the world.

The central theory that a work of art is essentially an idea which may (or may not) generate a physical form in any substance is exemplified in the work of Lawrence Weiner.

LAWRENCE WEINER (born 1940)

In 1968 Seth Siegelaub published a book by Weiner called *Statements*, on the copy-right page of which appears the sentence 'Certain Specific Statements are reproduced by kind permission of the people who own them'. Inside are a number of 'General Statements' and 'Specific Statements', one to a double page. They include in the former category 'A removal to the lathing or support wall of plaster or wall board from a wall' and in the latter, 'one quart exterior green enamel thrown on a brick wall.' The quotation in the Appendix, p. 24 (1968), indicates the status of these pieces and the other quotation further explains their intention. Many of the Statements indicate materials and processes which are closely akin to conventional works of art, 'One quart. . .' above seems to refer to the lawsuit between Whistler and Ruskin (who had accused Whistler of throwing a pot of paint in the public's face) or to Abstract Expressionism, but it is also the most rudimentary way to make a *painting*. Another type appears as a 'General Statement': 'A removal of an amount of earth from the ground. The intrusion into this hole of a standard processed material' and as a 'Specific Statement': 'One hole in the ground approximately one foot by one foot. One gallon water base white paint poured into this hole'. The intrusion of an object into a space as a work of art is a general definition of exhibiting works of art and the water paint particularizes the category of painting.

However, the central points are that Weiner was using materials as his subject matter and words as his medium, reversing the usual position, and that he left the execution to the owner, who may or may not carry it out but he asserts that any instance of carrying it out is as good as any other. That is, the quality does not reside in the particular manifestation and this manifestation is not a commercial commodity. The idea may have quality and may be sold (as ideas are sold in the form of patents, legal advice, musical scores etc.).

JOSEPH KOSUTH (born 1925)

Kosuth may be thought of as representing the extreme of departure from the art of manipulation of materials. The quotation in the Appendix, pp. 24–25, states his position very clearly, especially the passage in which he describes the regression from the level of abstraction 'the idea of an object' to the level 'the idea of an idea'. He gives a general title to his works 'Art as Idea as Idea', which makes the same point (Fig. 44). The word glossed there—'Radical'—is of course one that is in common use in relation to art. It is a term at the higher level of abstraction described above, that is it is a general term, comprehending a wide range of very different types of idea. Note that the definition of the word 'Radical' is not Kosuth's own; it is taken from a dictionary. This fact implies that the definition is itself a general one, current in the society in which the notion of art he deals with is current. Such borrowing from the public domain is the descendant of Warhol's borrowed newspaper images and before that of the prevailing American suspicion of deliberate composition that I have described so often.

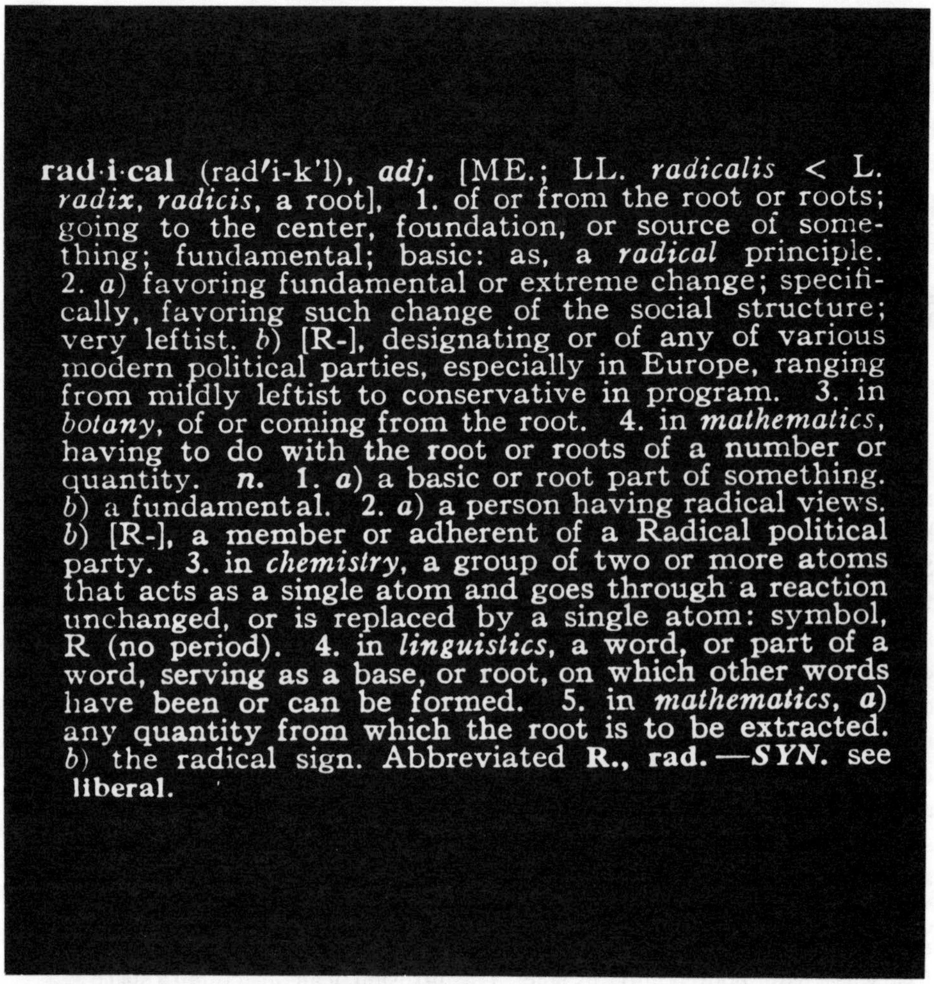

rad·i·cal (rad′i-k′l), *adj.* [ME.; LL. *radicalis* < L. *radix, radicis,* a root], 1. of or from the root or roots; going to the center, foundation, or source of something; fundamental; basic: as, a *radical* principle. 2. *a)* favoring fundamental or extreme change; specifically, favoring such change of the social structure; very leftist. *b)* [R-], designating or of any of various modern political parties, especially in Europe, ranging from mildly leftist to conservative in program. 3. in *botany,* of or coming from the root. 4. in *mathematics,* having to do with the root or roots of a number or quantity. *n.* 1. *a)* a basic or root part of something. *b)* a fundamental. 2. *a)* a person having radical views. *b)* [R-], a member or adherent of a Radical political party. 3. in *chemistry,* a group of two or more atoms that acts as a single atom and goes through a reaction unchanged, or is replaced by a single atom: symbol, R (no period). 4. in *linguistics,* a word, or part of a word, serving as a base, or root, on which other words have been or can be formed. 5. in *mathematics, a)* any quantity from which the root is to be extracted. *b)* the radical sign. Abbreviated **R., rad.** —*SYN.* see **liberal.**

Figure 44 Joseph Kosuth, *Titled* ('Art as Idea as Idea'), *RADICAL*, 1968, paper, 48 × 48 ins (Leo Castelli Gallery, New York; photo: Eric Pollitzer).

DOCUMENTATION

I have already given several instances of the substitution of some form of documentation for a crafted work of art—see Klein, Morris, Kosuth—and in succeeding pages you will find others. The distinction between object and document is to some extent an artificial or even paradoxical one. It is clear that as much craftsmanly attention can be given to the presentation of a photograph or text as to the carving of a piece of marble, especially if you consider not only the material elements of the document but also the medium in which it is to be presented: the gallery, the catalogue and even the society: a document is as much an object as a painting. Nevertheless the difference between them can be important even though it may be hardly more than a convention. A document is a means of referring to objects and events or of describing them but is not a 'representation' in the sense that a painting is. Documentation is also thought of as being, in principle at least, indefinitely replicable. Although documents may change hands at high prices (think of the value of the Magna Carta) any such value is not to be related to the quality of the document itself but to the event referred to, to a person associated with it, or to the accidental rarity of the item. To substitute symbolically the document for the object in the field of art, is to assert that the value, aesthetic or commercial, does not lie in the object or in the skill that creates the object but in the field of reference, or it may be completely arbitrary.

DOUGLAS HUEBLER (born 1924)

Huebler has used documents in this sense but also in a more active sense. As he says (Appendix, pp. 25–26). 'The documents . . . *make* the piece exist'; that is they direct the viewer, or rather the participant's attention or activity (Fig. 45). Here a spoken or

Figure 45 Douglas Huebler, two frames from *Duration Piece 6/14*, Bradford, Massachusetts, May 1970 (Courtesy of the artist).

written instruction directed the activity of the six people in the group. A second 'document', in the form of a word from among those listed, directed their thought during the taking of a photograph, which in turn acted as the instructions for forming the group next day. The exhibited piece consists of a description of that event, a description of the document itself (in the last two lines) and the set of words to be thought about. The viewer is likely to consider the words, to attempt to relate them to the sequence of photographs (which is impossible), and so to consider the structure of the piece. The character of the words which one knows the people in the photographs are thinking about, and the slight variations in the seven photographs, leads one to attempt to discern the personality of the members of the group.

A second piece comprises a print, each copy of which is given a number between 1 and 75. Each year, the owner of a print (say number 35) selects a photograph of himself taken that year and exchanges a copy with the current owners of the two prints with adjacent numbers (34 and 36) who have likewise chosen photographs of themselves. These photographs are then glued to the print. The print both instructs and documents. It represents a commitment on the part of the owner: it records the ageing of the owners, their choices of their own images and changes of ownership. It forms symbolic links within the community through the activity of exchange and cumulatively represents a cross section of the art world. In cases where the owner is a museum or other institution it raises the questions—who is the owner? how does he select his image? Huebler's work therefore represents the idea of locating art in the area of attention of the mind. The concept is related to Klein's 'Zones of Pictorial Sensibility', but instead of claiming rights, the documents serve to direct attention.

VICTOR BURGIN (born 1941)

Weiner, Kosuth and Huebler are American artists but there are analogies between their work and that of British and European contemporaries, no doubt largely as a result of the ever more complete exchange of information. Victor Burgin shares with the three named and other artists the use of words and photographs as a medium. Look at the piece which is transcribed in the Appendix, pp. 26–27. This is a series of phrases that were printed on thin card and spaced out round the walls of a large gallery, as if they were paintings. To view the whole piece one had to move round the room, standing in front of each card to read it. As in the case of Huebler, the viewer is directed to behave in this way by the work itself. It also directs his attention to himself and to other people and objects in the room and to his perception of them. By using a complex means of interlinking the position of the cards mentally and physically (you have constantly to go back and read earlier ones to check their exact wording) Burgin elicits a very different kind of thought and response from that elicited by Huebler. In a structure based on logic or set theory the relationship embeds certain intensely personal references: 'bodily acts', 'bodily contact', 'inner experience', etc.

Burgin's more recent work, such as *Lei Feng* (Fig. 46), has turned towards linguistics or semiotics in place of logic and to a political in place of a personal reference. References to the physical space have disappeared. Figure 46 is one of 9 frames, each of which is a copy of the same advertisement together with two passages of text, one of which is a Maoist parable that runs through the whole set; the other is a discussion of semiotics (the science of the meaning of signs.).

The Chinese anecdote shows a course of action in a new light or given a new value by the quotation of the authority of Mao, while the advertisement attempts to give a new value to a product, sherry, by associating it with symbols of achievement which are, however, not explicitly authoritative, but appear 'natural' in our society. The content of the piece concerns the control of people through the meaning given to verbal and pictorial images by those in power. All art operates by modifying the meaning of images but, in this instance, the process is laid bare.

The difference between language and iconic imagery is most marked in the case of the photograph. The linguistic sign bears an arbitrary relationship to its referent, the photographic image does not. There is no law in nature which dictates that the linguistic sign 'tree' (or 'l'arbre', or 'baum') should be associated with the thing with which it is in fact associated, this is a matter of cultural convention. In the case of the photograph on the other hand the image is in a sense caused by its referent. Just as there is a causal connection between the presence of an air-current and the direction in which a weathervane points, so a photo-sensitive emulsion *necessarily* registers the distribution of light to which it is exposed, leading Pierce to describe the photograph as a "quasi-predicate" of the light which stands to it as "quasi-subject".

The *chiaroscuro* of the photographic image replicates, *mutatis mutandis*, that present to the exposed film. What lines and volumes then emerge to our eye are related to their referents, as Volli has emphasised, strictly according to geometrical principles of projective transformation. In an ingenuous assumption the photograph is held to *re-produce* its object. However, the relationship between a photographic image and its referent is one of reproduction only to the extent that Christopher Wren's death-mask reproduces Christopher Wren. The photograph abstracts from, and mediates, the actual. For example, a photograph of three people grouped together may, in reality, have comprised a live model, a two-dimensional 'cut-out' figure, and a wax dummy. In the actual presence of such an assembly I would quickly know them for what they were. No such certainty accompanies my cognition of the photographic group. Barthes found in photography "...precious miracle, a reality from which we are sheltered," but if photographs shelter us from reality it is by nothing more ineffable than a shortage of information.

The young soldier Lei-Feng asks his instructor if he may be assigned to a combat mission. When refused he cannot hide his impatience.

Figure 46 Victor Burgin, *Lei Feng* (Tate Gallery, London).

ART AND LANGUAGE

Art and Language is a group of artists of fluctuating membership, including
Michael Baldwin, Terry Atkinson, Harrold Hurrell and David Bainbridge, whose
art arises out of and includes continuing discussion among themselves of art and of
anything that may be brought to bear on it. Art has always been affected by the concepts, ideas and thoughts that the artist derives from the society in which he lives and,

Figure 47 Art and Language,
Surf (Courtesy of *Art and
Language*, Banbury)

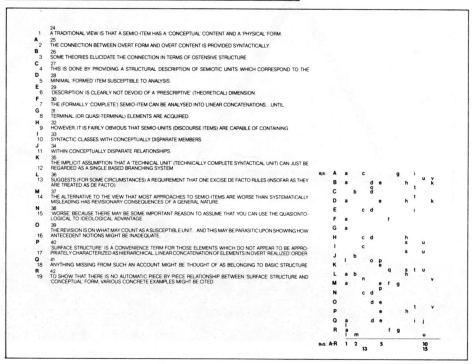

when a work is complete, it is perceived in terms that are affected equally by concepts which continually evolve as society changes. The work of art then effectively changes too. Art and Language brings this fact into the forefront of its work. More specifically, its strategy seems to be to dissolve or break up the conventional forms of words and the concepts which underlie them, so that the possibility of a new ideology and therefore a new art, may emerge. Such a process presents an analogy with Analytic Cubism, with the Constructivism of Lissitsky and with Abstract Expressionism. But by using words, it aims to get closer to the point at which concepts and ideologies are formed and so to go beyond the possibilities available to a painter.

The public part of the art consists of a journal, *Art and Language*, other written pieces, diagrams, filing systems and posters. Most of these are characterized by a dense and not completely intelligible style, mixing philosophic or scientific terminology with deliberately chatty, vulgar or aggressive phrases. Often the words or patterns of one convention of discourse are overlaid on another. This can be seen quite clearly in Figure 47 where the overall configuration is derived from Lissitsky but there are forms of tabulating and indexing by numbers.

As with Burgin, the intention is frankly revolutionary, to destroy the power of conservatism that is implicit in the control of symbols and meaning. A fully intelligible statement, like a fully intelligible painting, would be necessarily a conventional one.

JOHN LATHAM (born 1921)

The belief of the Art and Language group that art should be socially active is one that is shared by an older artist, John Latham. Figure 48 compares the assets of two companies for sale. One is a conventional commercial company, the other, the 'Artists' Placement Group', a company formed by Latham and his wife with others, to place artists in industrial concerns with a view to modify and eventually to change

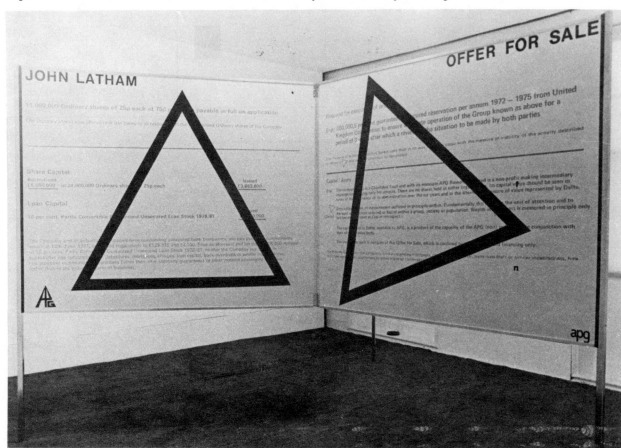

Figure 48 John Latham, *Offer for Sale*, November-December 1974 (Courtesy The Gallery, Lisson Street, London).

completely the conceptual bases on which they operate. Latham has come to identify more and more strongly the limits of conventional western science, technology and commerce which dominate our lives with space-based concepts, typified by the importance attached to physical objects. For this he proposes to substitute a time-based view, one which he sees as much more readily accessible to artists and one which takes serious and formal account of null events, that is, what does *not* exist, *not* happen, etc. There is some analogy with the following remark of the American artist Smithson, criticizing the cult of the art object:

> The mental process of the artist which takes *place* in time is disowned, so that a commodity value can be maintained by a system independent of the artist. Art, in this sense, is considered 'timeless' or a product of 'no time at all'; this becomes a convenient way to exploit the artist out of his rightful claim to his temporal processes. The arguments for the contention that time is unreal is a fiction of language, and not of the material of time or art.

HANS HAACKE (born 1936)

"Les Poseuses"
(small version)
$1,033,200 auction bid at Christie's, 1970, half share held by

Artemis S.A.

Incorporated April 2, 1970 in the Grand Duchy of Luxembourg; private holding company of subsidiaries incorporated in the United Kingdom (David Carritt, Ltd., London) and other countries. Invests and trades in works of the fine and decorative arts of all periods and cultures.

Inventory included Giovanni di Paolo, Rubens, Frans Hals, Rembrandt, Tiepolo, Veronese, Chardin, Goya, Ingres, Constable, Courbet, Cézanne, Sisley, Pissarro, Picasso, Feininger, Klee, Kandinsky, de Chirico, Moore, de Kooning, Gorky, Michael Heizer, Greek and Roman statues, Luba sculpture, Nepalese bronze, Egyptian jar, Lomellini Silver.

Collaborating art dealers include E.V. Thaw & Co., New York; Fourcade, Droll, Inc., New York; R.M. Light & Co., Boston; Heinz Berggruen & Cie., Paris; Heinz Herzer & Co., Munich; P. & D. Colnaghi, London; Heim, London; Lefevre, London; Fischer Fine Art, London.

Works sold among others to National Gallery, Washington; Cleveland Museum; Norton Simon Foundation; Ashmolean Museum, Oxford.

Board of Directors
Baron Léon Lambert, Chairman since 1970. Chairman of Compagnie Bruxelles Lambert.

Eugene Victor Thaw, managing director since 1974. Head of E.V. Thaw & Co. Private dealer. 1970-72 President of Art Dealers Association of America, Inc.

David Carritt, since 1970. Head of David Carritt Ltd., Artemis subsidiary in London. Old Master expert, formerly with Christie's, London.

Count Christian zu Salm-Reifferscheidt, 1970-73. Art historian, expert in antique art. Former curator of Bavarian State Museum, Munich. Deceased.

Philippe R. Stoclet, since 1970. Investment banker, Brussels. Former representative of Loeb, Rhoades & Co., New York, investment bank. Descendant of Alphonse Stoclet, international railroad builder; important collector, who commissioned architect Josef Hoffman of "Wiener Werkstatten" to build Palais Stoclet, Brussels.

Count Artur Strachwitz, since 1970. Born 1905. Brother-in-law of Prince of Liechtenstein. Former cultural attaché at Brussels Embassy of German Federal Republic.

Baron Alexis de Rédé, since 1970. Financial consultant, collector. Among major beneficiaries of inheritance of his late friend, Arturo Lopez, South American financier. Lives in 17th century Hôtel Lambert, Paris, rue St. Louis en Ile, now owned by Baron Guy de Rothschild, a friend.

Walter Barreiss, since 1973. Born 1919, Tübingen, Germany. Chairman of family business Schachenmeyr, Mann & Cie. GmbH., Salach, Germany, yarn factory. Chairman of Cobar Industries, Inc. Served in U.S. Army in World War II. Married to Molly Stimson, cousin of Henry L. Stimson, late US Secretary of War. Collector. Member collection committee for 20th century art and chairman of Gallery Association of Bavarian State Museum, Munich. Trustee of Museum of Modern Art, New York, 1964-73, acting director 1969-70. Lives Munich and Greenwich, Conn.

Heinz Berggruen, since 1974. Head of Paris art gallery, Heinz Berggruen & Cie..

Art Advisory Board
Baron and Baroness Élie de Rothschild, 1970-73; Prof. Abraham Hammacher, 1970-73; Douglas Cooper, 1971-73; Roderic Thesiger, 1971-73; Heinz Herzer, since 1971; Count Cesare Cicogna Mozzoni, 1972-73; Valentine Abdy, since 1974.

Holding Company and Subsidiaries

Year	consolidated profit	total assets	assets works of art at cost
1970-71	$ 43,042	$ 5,431,299	$2,207,680
1971-72	641,992	5,703,195	3,676,507
1972-73	778,448	8,010,350	5,787,507
1973-74	733,397	10,256,991	7,864,400

Authorized capital: 1,000,000 shares of $10 nominal value per share. Issued capital: 413,025 shares of $10 each: $4,130,250 (Oct. 1974).

Figure 49 Hans Haacke, *Artemis S.A.*, panel from Seurat's *Les Poseuses*, 1888–1975, 14 panels, ink on paper, 30 × 20 ins plus reproduction of the painting (Courtesy of John Weber Gallery, New York).

The work of Hans Haacke has been consistently about systems or, more accurately, he has made, exploited or demonstrated systems. In his earlier pieces of this type the systems are 'natural': the evaporation and condensation of water in an enclosed transparent box, the growth of grass under certain conditions, the incubation and emergence of chicks from the egg, etc. Later ones involve social systems, including invariably (by implication) the viewers and the galleries or museums in which they are shown (see Appendix, pp. 27–28). In the event the work that he was preparing for the Guggenheim, mentioned in this text, turned out to be a documentation of the largely slum property owned by a company of which certain of the Trustees of that museum were directors. The museum refused to show this and there was a considerable flurry in the art world and the media. This refusal and the arguments that arose from it were of course an essential part of the system documented and created by the artist, even though he could not have entirely foreseen the result. I feel that from his point of view the upshot (like that of Tinguely's *Homage to New York*) was the best possible, because it demonstrates the negative side of the attitude described by Emily Genauer at the end of the Haacke text (Appendix, p. 28).

Later pieces by Haacke have been less conspicuously political, or rather, they depend for their political effect on the response of the viewer to a presentation which has a less obviously loaded iconography than slum tenements. These include the documentation of the ownership of paintings, which, having been sold for small sums by the artist, change hands at ever more enormous prices among people whose positions of economic power, are included in the documentations (Fig. 49). Still more recent pieces are tablets engraved with quotations about art and patronage by the same class of person. Clearly, if you regard these remarks as magnanimous, you may see the work as favourable to the speakers and to their views; if you regard them as empty or hypocritical, you will see the piece as a social statement of the radical left. I should point out that the great majority of political art has this type of ambiguity: think of Velasquez's portraits of King Philip, or Courbet's *Stone Breakers*.

JOHN HILLIARD (born 1945)

This artist is representative of a number who have made works which are reflexive, in that they reveal systematically the process by which the work was made and nothing else. In his case, the medium is generally photography. For example, one piece consists of a set of photographs of the camera which is taking the photographs, reflected in a mirror. The set includes every combination of aperture and exposure time available on that camera and these can be read in a second mirror. The prints are then set out in a paradigmatic manner, which demonstrates the range of image produced by the variations in the internal state of the instrument. A later type of work, comprises four copies of the same photograph, cut in different ways, so that one part, usually a figure, is common to the whole set. The figure appears in a different context in each print, depending on what else is included, and a different title is given to each. Such a work reveals the implications of the fact that part of the process of making a photograph is to include a certain zone and to exclude the rest. No photograph can, of course, include the whole context of what the camera is pointed at (compare this with de Kooning's 'no environment', p. 14), but we are still inclined to see photographs as representing the 'truth', even though the context gives meaning to every phenomenon.

HANNE DARBOVEN (born 1941)

One of the characteristics of much conceptual art has been the systematic working out of a predetermined scheme. Antecedents may be found in Stella and LeWitt (pp. 35 and 68) and, before that, in Constructivist artists like Morellet and Kenneth Martin (see TV Programme 10). The most extreme example is perhaps the German artist Hanne Darboven, whose early work was in the constructive tradition. Even-

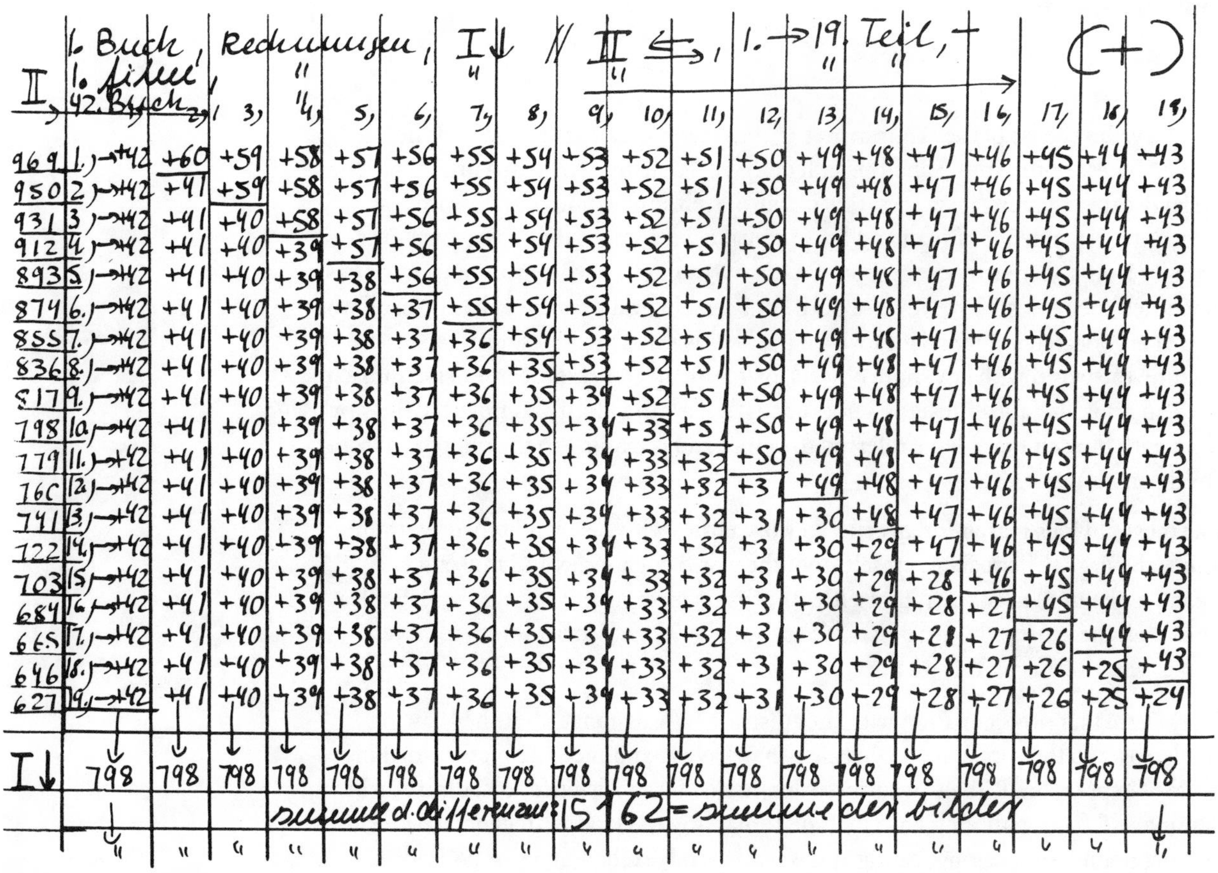

Figure 50 Hanne Darboven, first plate in De Europa exhibition, April 1972, ink on paper (Courtesy of John Weber Gallery, New York).

tually the systems of simple arithmetic operations which she had used as the basis of this work, became self-sufficient, and she has spent the years since 1967 carrying out such operations, which are bound in books and supplied with indices (Fig. 50). Here the number 42, which makes up the whole of the first column, is progressively reduced to 41, 40 . . . in succeeding columns, but the upper part of each column is replaced by a progressively lengthening series of numbers, 60, 59 . . . which are those required to keep the sum of numbers in the column constant at 798. It can be seen that these are always the number in the lower part of the column, plus 19, which is the number of horizontal lines of figures. Darboven seems to do this for no other purpose than the pleasure of the work, work that self-evidently consumes a lot of her time. Indeed it can be thought of as taking up and marking out essentially the whole time and, therefore, the whole life of the artist. It is an identification of life with *doing* rather than with purpose and also an assertion that art is possible without any purpose or function other than the drive of the artist.

Land Art and Body Art

The prevailing sense of the arbitrariness of the conventional art media and the restrictiveness of the studio and the gallery, have led many artists to work in, or with, the landscape. In many instances, this has also been a reflection of the awareness of the interdependence of man and his physical environment that has grown ever stronger from the mid 1960s; artists have always wanted to make art out of what has concerned them most. The obverse of the same ecological awareness has been another kind of art, located in the artist's own body. That is, the artist does not wish to 'pollute' the world with any more objects, or to use up any resources outside himself. Such an art is also a manifestation of the artist's wish to identify completely the work of art with himself that I have referred to before and is explicit in the quotation from Smithson above, p. 81.

The most obvious reason for an artist to work either with his own body or with the land is the urge to dissociate himself from the world of galleries and museums. A second is the urge to concern himself with what is most primitive and inescapable. Almost all the artists who are described as 'Body' or 'Land' artists seem to have a strong sense of magic or ritual.

They share that preoccupation with the Abstract Expressionists but they can get much closer to the core of magic because they have abandoned the picture-making mode of expression. Rituals in cultures dominated by subsistence agriculture or by hunting and food-gathering have included: marking the land with geometric forms, walking boundaries, fasting, eating and wasting food, exchanging symbolic gifts, painting or mutilating the body, miming birth, copulation and death, as well as simulating the exchange of sexual and other roles. The means used include: costumes and masks, the substitution of parts for the whole, or of man-made or naturally occurring resemblances like the mandrake root. All of these can be found in the art which I am describing in this section.

JOSEF BEUYS (born 1921)

Troels Andersen has given this account of one of Beuys's (pronounced 'Boyce') 'actions':

> At first glance he belongs to the fantastic characters somewhere between clown and gangster. In action he is changed, absorbed into his performance, intense and suggestive. He uses very simple symbols. His performance was the 32nd section from the *Siberian Symphony*, and lasted an hour and a half. The introductory motif was 'the division of the cross'. Kneeling, Beuys slowly pushed two small crosses which were lying on the floor towards a blackboard; on each cross was a watch with an adjusted alarm. On the board he drew a cross which he then half erased; underneath he wrote 'Eurasia'.

> The remainder of the piece consisted of Beuys maneuvering, along a marked line, a dead rabbit whose ears and legs were extended by long, thin black wooden poles. When the rabbit was on his shoulders, the poles touched the floor. Beuys moved from the wall to the board where he deposited the rabbit. On the way back, three things happened; he sprinkled white powder between the rabbit's legs, put a thermometer in its mouth, and blew into a tube. Afterwards he turned to the board with the erased cross and allowed the rabbit to twitch his ears while he himself allowed one foot, which was tied to an iron plate, to float over a similar plate, on the floor.

> This the main content of the action. The symbols are completely clear and they

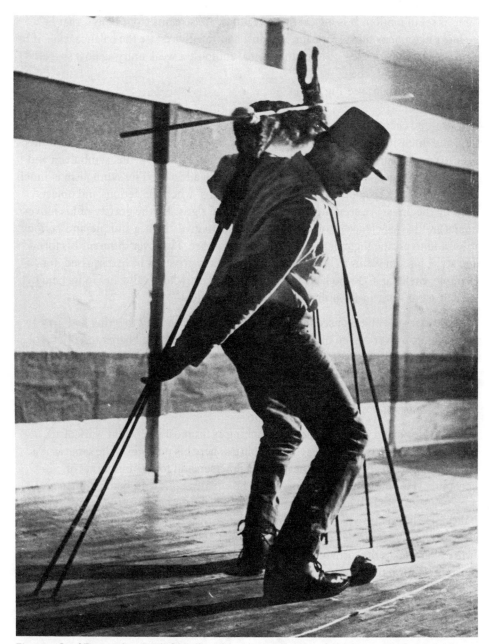

Figure 51 Josef Beuys, photograph from 'Eurasia' action, 1966 (Kaare Per Johannesen, Copenhagen).

are all translatable. The division of the cross is the split between East and West, Rome and Byzantium. The half cross is the United Europe and Asia, to which the rabbit is on its way. The iron plate on the floor is a metaphor—it is hard to walk and the ground is frozen. The three interruptions on the way back signify the elements snow, ice, wind. All this is understandable only when the word 'Siberia' is caught. But the symbols' significance is of secondary importance. Beuys is performing no cultural philosophical sketch. That is made clear by his extreme concentration. A man who spends himself to such an extent before an audience does this not only for the sake of certain rules set up for this particular situation. His actions require perspective and are penetrating because they are part of a larger context. . . He uses the expressions 'counterspace' and 'countertime' to indicate the psychic factors which make it possible to realize such a relationship to and experience of the materially given space. When the legs of the rabbit quiver, the poles sway out of their position—as they do incessantly during this exciting trip—and when he has great difficulty bringing them back to the proper position —for a moment then, our relationship to space breaks down. Something within

85

us is set in motion. It is logical that sweat flows in streams from Beuys, that he looks like a person in great pain. He must continually restate the balance, even if he stands on only one leg. . . Man and animal compose a weak unity against space which surrounds them.
(Andersen, 1966; see Fig. 51.)

This is quite characteristic in its use of the body of a dead animal, in the extreme slowness and intensity of the action and in the fact that there is a perfectly legible symbolism to every element. Andersen plays down the importance of this symbolism and it is true that it is not used by Beuys to construct an allegory. The symbolism is much closer to that of a religious ritual whose power is lost when the actions and objects used by the priest are seen merely as conventional signs. By the gravity of his movements and by his choice of objects, Beuys seeks to give them a unique and serious value and to escape the 'relativism' of western culture. However different his forms and style, his aim seems to be similar to that of many artists (I have discussed, for example, Stella, p. 61) who have tried to evolve an art whose value lies in its being what it is and not in its utility in some other context.

In some cases the objects used in Beuys's actions have been put together and preserved as an art work, even though the materials, including dead hares and often, cooking fat, are evidently impermanent, difficult to manage (to keep clean for example) and more or less disagreeable to many people. These facts in themselves seem to draw attention to the reality of the symbol which I have mentioned, if only because without great necessity one would not attempt to use them.

Beuys has for many years regarded his teaching as his most important work of art. More recently he has also been active in politics: here his position is the same as it is in his 'actions': to give value to the individual person and to the unique act or encounter. He emphasizes freedom, which he equates both with being human and with being an artist: 'without art man is inconceivable in *physiological* terms' (my italics). He has set up a party whose aim is to give the creative role to the man in the street and no longer to delegate it to professional politicians or leaders. This perennial 'work of art' takes the form of almost endless discussions in galleries or elsewhere, the most direct form of communication, but he has also helped to organize a series of centres like small shops in various cities to which anyone may come to offer proposals, criticism or questions on any aspect of social and political life and to receive help and information.

Anarchism of various kinds has been common to many artists in the last hundred years. It may be seen as an extension of the artists' asserted right to represent the world in his own individual way. However, only recently have certain small, rich and highly developed states, such as Holland and Sweden, come to take account of such concepts in their political institutions, giving artists and other citizens direct access to public media and government organizations.

DENNIS OPPENHEIM (born 1938)

Speaking of the origins of his 'Land' art, Oppenheim said in an interview (Oppenheim, 1970, p. 50): 'to me a piece of sculpture inside a room is a disruption of interior space'. He began to make sculptures, not by adding something to the land, but by cutting something into it. Often this was in ice or snow or in some other ephemeral surface. Often the configuration he cut was a man-made pattern transferred from its original material and context—the ground plan of his dealer's gallery, a time-line from a map. In 1970 he began to work more with his own body, feeling that there should be an echo in the body of the work on the land. This is in itself a similar idea to that of the transfers just mentioned, and is, of course, more distantly related to the ideal of 'representation' in painting. However, there is a difference, in that the quality of the representation is not in question. It is simply that an alien concept is printed onto the chosen living field, whether land or body, whereas in a painting the canvas is not thought of as being alive or of responding actively to what is done to it.

One of the most simple, *Reading Position for a Second Degree Burn*, consisted of the artist lying in the sun for five hours with a book on his chest so that his body (except where the book had been) was severely reddened by the sun. This is an allegory of nature painting the artist instead of the artist painting nature. In more recent works the idea of interchange is taken further; these consist of one person drawing a complex line on the back of another while that person attempts to reproduce the line on a piece of paper. The people concerned are his own family (Fig. 52); this, like the use of his own body, seems to signify the maximum of identity and interchange between artist and work of art, so that the hierarchy of artist, work of art and materials is broken down. Such a position seems to have a clear social content. A sense of identity and of equality of status is to replace the sense of doing and being done to.

Figure 52 Dennis Oppenheim, *Two-stage Transfer Drawing*, Dennis Oppenheim to Erik Oppenheim (returning to a past state). Artist's text: 'As I run a marker along Erik's back, he attempts to duplicate the movement on the wall. My activity stimulates kinetic response from his sensory system. I am, therefore, *drawing through him*. Sensory retardation or disorientation makes up the discrepancy between the two drawings, and could be seen as elements that are activated during this procedure. Because Erik is my offspring, and we share similar biological ingredients, his back (as surface) can be seen as an immature version of my own . . . in a sense, I make contact with a past state.'

RICHARD LONG (born 1945)

Long carries out three main kinds of works: the first are activities in outdoor places and their results, the second are types of documentation referring to these, the third are made in or for galleries but are made of the kinds of materials he uses in the first. In each case the methods and materials are of the simplest and the most natural, that is, they are as closely as possible adapted to the place or medium. Essentially he makes marks on the land. They vary simply in the amount of work needed to make them, in the degree to which the land is disturbed and in the degree to which they can be perceived. A line may be made by walking over grass: if he walks over it repeatedly it can be seen for some time, if he walks only once it can probably not be seen, but may

be known from a map. On a beach covered by stones, a figure can be made by arrang-
ing some of the stones in a square. This can be perceived because it is characteristic
of man to make squares, while the action of the sea produces a nearly random distribution; when the tide rises it will restore the sea's order. In its great simplicity, a work
like this reveals certain basic but important truths, and points to the infinitely complex processes of man and nature. Long is careful not to do too much. A work which is
too complex or contains too much information seems to contain thought within its
own system, but one which is simple, provided it is placed at an important nexus in
the human understanding, can be magical. It contains implications over the widest
range as a result of its rightness in a smaller range.

In the case of *October 1969 (Four Squares)* (Fig. 53) what is presented to people (other
than those who might have seen Long passing by on those days) is a map with four
squares concentrically drawn on it. This is a 'natural' way to arrange four squares but
it also makes it clear without need for any dimensions that the squares are in the
proportion 1:2:3:4. A time is also given for each square which the caption identifies as
the time taken to walk around it. It can easily be deduced that there is not a constant
proportion between distance and time so the time dimension is elastic in relation to the
space. The reasons for this can be imagined but are not stated: it must have been that
the longer distances were more tiring and that the terrain varies. The walks covered a
specific area on the edge of Salisbury plain that can be identified from a larger map.
The squares, though rectilinear in plan, were, as walked, very irregular in elevation
and in incident, as the map indicates. The superimposition of a regular pattern on the
form of the land which can be deduced from the map brings to mind the physical
character of the surface of the latter. The smallest square is over a fairly flat, low and
undifferentiated landscape, while the second largest runs close to the road and villages
to the south (right) and the largest climbs and runs along an escarpment (also right)
overlooking the whole area covered: the whole sculpture.

Nevertheless, this piece is not essentially autobiographical: there is no indication of
the weather, though the date is given; there is no indication of the order in which the
squares were walked, though it seems natural that they should have been in ascending
order of size; there is no indication of any incident that took place or of any specific
feelings on the part of the artist. There is only the concept of such a walk, the particular place, the times and the possibilities and combinations of these. The artist under-
took them and also the marking of the map in the frame of mind of a person making a
painting or sculpture by 'touching the earth', and so subtly, taking possession for a
moment, but without excluding anyone else. He was there and has gone just as
Constable was in Dedham Vale and has gone, has touched his canvas and has gone.

Exercise

What do you consider to be the relationship of documentation to the activities of
artists recorded in such documentation? In what sense is the documentation to be
regarded as art?

Discussion

In some cases (e.g. Beuys) the documentation relates to what was in the first place a
public manifestation—both are public works of art and the documentation, although
it may have in some respects the character of a souvenir, is made up of objects that
are substantial and not very different from those used directly by assemblage artists
(like Rauschenberg in the 50s and early 60s) to construct works of art that can only
be regarded as self-contained. The emphasis that Beuys places on the inherent meaning of objects and animals justifies his use of them equally in either mode.

In the case of an artist like Long or Oppenheim there is a sense that a work in the
documentary mode, although it is itself created as a work of art and has the power of a

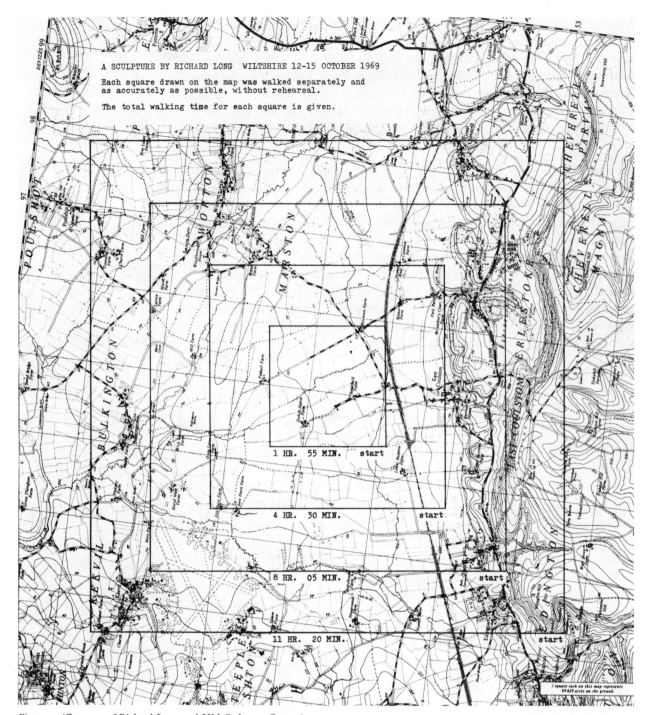

A SCULPTURE BY RICHARD LONG WILTSHIRE 12-15 OCTOBER 1969

Each square drawn on the map was walked separately and
as accurately as possible, without rehearsal.

The total walking time for each square is given.

1 HR. 55 MIN.   start

4 HR. 30 MIN.   start

8 HR. 05 MIN.   start

11 HR. 20 MIN.   start

Figure 53 (Courtesy of Richard Long and HM Ordnance Survey).

work of art for anyone who contemplates it receptively, remains to a degree secondary. Its power depends on an imaginative reconstruction of the activity recorded or indicated. This condition is not unlike that of any representational painting or sculpture, for that too is the product of a particular or generalized encounter between the artist and the physical world which has to be in some way intuited by the viewer of the work of art. You do not have to know the sitter to appreciate a portrait but you have to have experience of the range of variation of human form and of the way it works (especially how it expresses itself) in order to respond to the specifics of the painting. This reaction is of course virtually instantaneous so that we have a sense of illusion rather than of scrutinising the record of a prolonged encounter between artist and nature, even though one of the conventional values of a painting is that it is such a record. Cézanne was one of the few artists who painted pictures where the encounter with nature remains inescapably present in the finished painting to the degree that I, at any rate, feel that however great the painting (and that is very great indeed) it is never either complete or as complex or as poignant as the original encounter. There is nevertheless an obviously profound difference between Cézanne's painting and Long's or Oppenheim's photographs or maps. The latter are deliberately distanced from the artist's personal experience that it is not possible to confuse them. The media used are those we associate with objectivity rather than with the artist's original hand. The function is to point to a truth or reality without allowing the viewer to become fixated on the object before him.

Artists like Beuys, Oppenheim and Long illustrate the strength of the urge to extend the aesthetic response from paint on canvas to anything that the artist can touch or point to, including his own person and society at large. Similarly, the artists' mode has been extended from representation to any activity he can accomplish, including thinking, speaking and writing, as well as all kinds of physical transforming and transposing. This direction has been latent in the whole of twentieth-century art, if not apparent. Its ancestors include collage, ready-mades and artists' polemics like those of the Futurists and Vorticists but also the more distant 'right' of the artist to define his own art, from Michelangelo's intransigence, to Constable, who, according to Professor Lawrence Gowing, established 'The conception of art as whatever artists are obstinate enough to persist in . . .'

Recommended Reading and References

Those marked with an asterisk are recommended further reading.

Andersen, T. (1966) in *Bildkunst*, Copenhagen, No. 4.

*Battcock, G. (1966) (ed.) *The New Art*, Dutton.

Caro, A. (1972) Interview, in *Artforum*, June 1972.

*Greenberg, C. (1961) *Art and Culture*, Beacon Press.

*Henry, A. (1974) *Environments and Happenings*, Thames and Hudson.

Hess, T. B. (1971) *Barnett Newman*, exhibition catalogue, Museum of Modern Art, New York.

*Lippard, L. (1966) (ed.) *Pop Art*, Thames and Hudson.

*Lippard, L. (1973) (ed.) *Six Years: The Dematerialization of the Art Object*, Studio Vista.

Oppenheim, D. (1970) Interview, in *Avalanche*, Fall 1970.

*Rose, B. (1967) *American Art since 1900*, Thames and Hudson.

*Sandler, I. (1970) *The Triumph of American Painting: A History of Abstract Expressionism*, Pall Mall Press.

Seckler, D. (1962) 'Frontiers of Space, An Interview with Barnett Newman', in *Art in America*, Summer 1962.

Seitz, W. (1962) *Arshile Gorky*, exhibition catalogue, Museum of Modern Art, New York.

Whitechapel Gallery (1963) *Anthony Caro*, exhibition catalogue, Whitechapel Gallery, London.

Plate 1   Arshile Gorky, *The Betrothal II*, 1947, oil, 50¾ × 38 ins (Collection of Whitney Museum of American Art, New York).

Plate 2   Willem de Kooning, *Woman I*, 1950–52, oil, 75⅞ × 58 ins (Collection Museum of Modern Art, New York).

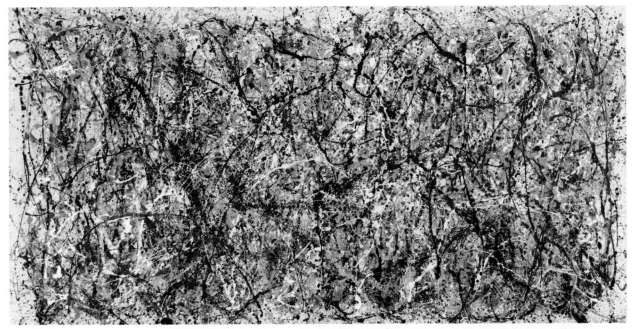

Plate 3 Jackson Pollock, *One (Number 31)*, 1950, oil and enamel on canvas, 106 × 209⅝ ins (Collection Museum of Modern Art, New York, gift of Sidney Janis).

Plate 4 Jackson Pollock, detail from *Blue Poles*, 1953, oil, Duco and aluminium paint on canvas, 83 × 192½ ins, detail approximately 10 × 15 ins (National Gallery of Australia; photo: courtesy of Thames and Hudson from Bryan Robertson, *Jackson Pollock*, 1960).

Plate 5 Clyfford Still, *Painting*, 1951, oil, 94 × 83 ins (Collection Museum of Modern Art, New York, Blanchette Rockefeller Fund).

Plate 6 Barnett Newman, *Vir Heroicus Sublimis*, 1950, 1951, oil, 95⅜ × 213⅛ ins (Collection Museum of Modern Art, New York, gift of Mr and Mrs Ben Heller; photo: Eric Pollitzer).

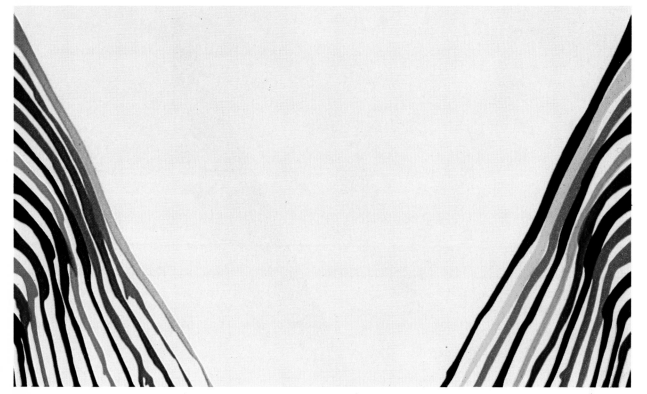

Plate 7   Morris Louis, *Sigma*, 1961, oil, 103 × 170½ ins (Collection Eugene M. Schwartz).

Plate 8   Anthony Caro, *Early One Morning*, 1962, acrylic on metal, 114 × 244 × 132 ins (Tate Gallery, London).

Plate 10 Jasper Johns, *Three Flags*, oil, 31 × 45½ × 5 ins (Collection of Mrs Burton Tremaine).

Plate 11 Robert Rauschenberg, *Bed*, 1955, combine painting (various materials on canvas), 74 × 31 ins (Collection Mr and Mrs Leo Castelli, New York).

Plate 12 Richard Hamilton, *Just What is it Makes Today's Homes So Different, So Appealing?*, 1956, collage, $10\frac{1}{4} \times 9\frac{3}{4}$ ins (Kunsthalle, Tubingen).

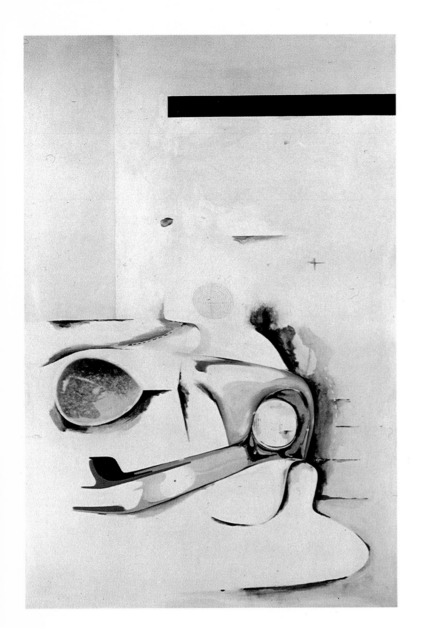

Plate 13 Richard Hamilton, *Hommage à Chrysler Corp.*, 1957, oil and metal foil collage on panel, 48 × 32 ins (Collection E. J. Power).

Plate 14 Richard Smith, *Staggerlee*, 1963, oil, 89 × 89 ins (Peter Stuyvesant Foundation).

Plate 15 David Hockney, *Christopher Isherwood and Don Bachardy*, 1968, oil (Kasmin Gallery, London).

Plate 16 Roy Lichtenstein, *Drowning Girl*, 1963, oil and synthetic polymer paint on canvas, $67\frac{5}{8} \times 66\frac{3}{4}$ ins (Collection Museum of Modern Art, New York, Philip Johnson Fund and gift of Mr and Mrs Bagley Wright).

Plate 17 Andy Warhol, *Marilyn*, 1967, colour print, 36 × 36 ins (Tate Gallery, London).